PIVOTAL POWER

Leveraging Your Energy, Authority, Influence and Ability to Do the Impossible

Loren Murfield, Ph.D.

Pivotal Power

© 2021 Loren O. Murfield, Ph.D.

All rights reserved. No part of this book may be used or reproduced in any manner whatsoever without the written permission of the publisher, Murfield International, Inc. Printed in the United States of America. For information, contact Loren Murfield, Ph.D. at Loren@MurfieldCoaching.com

Dedication

To those who aspire, may you find your power to do what you thought impossible and to do what others never imagined.

Books by Dr. Murfield

Business & Professional Development Books

Pivotal Apathy: Secrets to Letting Go of Things That Don't Matter (2021)

Pivotal Business: 8 Gears to Lead Your Business from a Chevette to a Corvette. (2007, 3rd Ed. 2020)

Pivotal Compassion: 4 Strategic Steps to Unleash the Ultimate Performance, Production, and Profits in Traumatic Times. Lisa & Loren Murfield (2nd Ed. 2018)

Pivotal Conversations with My Future Self: Book 1: Identifying the Prize Inside (2020)

Pivotal Conversations with My Future Self: Book 2: Valuing, Owning, Sharing and Secrets to Becoming a Disruptive Leader (2020)

Pivotal Engagement: 4 Steps to Create an Innovative Culture. Loren & Lisa Murfield. (2019)

Pivoting From Stupid: How to Make S.M.A.R.T. Decisions and Stop Being S.T.U.P.I.D. in Times of Opportunity (2020)

Pivotal Leaders: 21 Principles to Continually Thinking Bigger and Reaching Higher in the Next Normal. (2021)

Pivotal Listening: Building Your Breakthrough Team with Compassion, Strategy and Power. (2020)

Pivotal Living and Working. (2021)

Pivotal Networking: 5 Steps to Build Great Relationships, Increase Sales, and Seize Your Best Opportunities. (2020)

Pivotal Opportunities: Utilizing Your 6 Senses to Sense and Seize Opportunities When You Need Them Most (2nd Ed. 2018)

Pivotal Paradigm Shift: Making Money in Tough Times by Asking One Disruptive Question. (3rd Ed. 2020)

Pivotal Power: How to Leverage the 4 Critical Elements of Cutting-Edge Teams. (2021)

Pivotal Procrastination: (2023) How I ALMOST Made $1 Million: Your Guide to Take the Right Action at the Right Time. (2023)

Pivotal Thinking: 4 Types of Thinking to Create Your Breakthrough. Thinking Bigger to Make Smart Decisions and Avoid Unnecessary Problems. (20202024)

Your Pivotal Prize Inside: The Parable of a Little Boy with a Big Idea (2019)

Legacy Books
Just One More: How I Ran 6 Marathons in the Year I Turned 68 (2024)
Too Tough To Quit: 12 Inspirational Stories from the 2023 Chicago Marathon Back of the Pack Runners (2023)
Medal Monday: My Quest to Run 50 Marathons in 50 States in 50 Weeks 5 Years after Being Shot 5 Times. With Aaron Burros. (2022)
Pitchfork to Ph.D.: The Journey from "I AM a Chore Boy Follower" to "I AM a Disruptive Leader. (2021)
10 Minutes of Insanity. Coauthored with Heisman Winner Johnny Rodgers (2016)
Humble Homesteaders: A South Dakota Story of Integrity (2010)

Spiritual Books
Turbulent Serenity: Unleash Your Ultimate Spiritual Life (2011)
Heavenly Opportunities: Unleash Your Ultimate Relationship with God (2011)
God's Workmanship: Unleash the Ultimate Spiritual Relationship with Ourselves (2011)
Fellow Travelers: Unleash Your Ultimate Spiritual Relationship with Others (2011)
Resurrection: The Ultimate Opportunity (2011)

Meditation Books (to be released 2023+)
Meditations from the National Parks: Introduction, (2023)
Awe: Meditations from the Grand Canyon National Park (2024)
History: Meditations from the Great Smoky Mountains National Park (2024)
Journey: Meditations from the Bryce Canyon Mountains National Park (2024)
Majesty: Meditations from Mt. Rainier National Monument (2024)
Mystery: Meditations from Great Smoky Mountains National Park (2024)
Measured: Meditations from Wind Cave National Park (20243)
Mystery: Meditations from the Great Smoky Mountains National Park (2024)
Opportunities: Meditations from Olympic National Park (2024)
Power: Meditations from Mt. St. Helens National Monument (2024)
Protection: Meditations from the Everglades National Park (2024)
Reach Higher: Meditations from Rocky Mountain National Park (2024)
Strength: Meditations from Zion National Park (2024)
Surprise: Meditations from the Badlands National Park (2024)
Unbridled: Meditations from the North Cascades National Parks (2024)
Ultimate: Meditations from Yosemite National Park (2024)
Vulnerable: Meditations from Glacier National Park (2024)
Wonder: Meditations from Yellowstone National Park (2024)

TABLE of CONTENTS

INTRODUCTION: POWERFUL OPPORTUNITIES 9
PIVOTAL OPPORTUNITIES 23
    Checklist: Pivotal Opportunities 27
PIVOTAL CHOICES 29
    Checklist: Power in Choosing 34
DEFINING POWER 35
    Checklist: Pivoting from Obsolete Power 49
TYPES OF POWER 51
    Checklist: Types of Power 57
4 ELEMENTS of POWER 59
    Checklist: Elements of Power 62
ENERGY 63
    Checklist: Energy 75
ABILITY 77
    Checklist: Ability 82
    Self-Concept 83
    Checklist: Self-Concept 85
    Self-Awareness 87
    Checklist: Self-Awareness 89
    Self-Esteem 91
    Checklist: Self-Esteem 96
    Self-Disclosure 97
    Checklist: Self-Disclosure 104
    Checklist: Ability 106
AUTHORITY 107

Checklist: Authority	113
INFLUENCE	115
Checklist: Influence	119
Checklist: Pivotal Leadership Power	120
POWERFUL COMMUNICATION	121
Checklist: Pivotal Power Communication	125
CONCLUSION	129
REFERENCES	131
PIVOTAL LIVING AND WORKING SERIES	133
MEDITATIONS from the NATIONAL PARKS SERIES	133
VIDEO COURSES and SERIES	135
COMING SOON	136
ABOUT the AUTHOR	137

INTRODUCTION: POWERFUL OPPORTUNITIES

"As we look ahead into the next century, leaders will be those who empower others."
Bill Gates

We stand on the threshold of phenomenal opportunities. Never before have we had as many great opportunities at our fingertips than we do today. Unfortunately, too many are distracted by things that aren't important. We miss fantastic opportunities for our ultimate achievement because we cared about what didn't matter. We are distracted at the exact time we need to be focused.

There is an easier way to get what you ultimately want.

Leaders have been clamoring for power and control for centuries. They have waged physical, financial, and emotional war in their quest to attain advantage in every arena, including the political, industrial, cultural, academic, and religious. In their mind, the best, or easiest way, to secure the ultimate results was to wield power.

Unfortunately, they were mistaken, mistaken, and misinformed. They don't know the secret to pivotal leadership.

I've written this book to help you become pivotal, continually shifting to seize your ultimate, personal opportunities and do what you and others never thought possible. This book focuses on developing your individual power while my previous book, *Pivotal Engagement* focuses on developing your organizational leadership.

I have built my catalog of books around the opportunity to become pivotal and do what we never imagined. We unleash the ultimate when we learn to continually shift our perspective, attitude, knowledge, and skills, we set goals far beyond what we or others expected. We think and act on a higher plane. We learn to zig when other zag to do amazing things. In the end, we wonder wish we had made the pivot sooner.

The Problem

Too many of us are settling for ordinary results when we could do what we never thought possible. We doubt ourselves and cannot believe that we could be the ones to do something that others haven't considered possible. We cannot imagine how we could exceed our own expectations, let alone the expectations of others because we don't appreciate or leverage the power we already have.

We live in a world that is changing rapidly and radically. We often don't feel as if we have enough time to continually think bigger and reach higher to seize the incredible opportunities. We feel overwhelmed and doubt we have the power to step up. We wonder if we have enough power to survive, much less thrive.

The problem is that we haven't learned to think bigger and, therefore, don't appreciate the power we currently hold. Unfortunately, we miss incredible opportunities because we didn't think we had the energy, ability, authority, or influence. We assumed wrong.

Another problem is that we've been taught that power comes with position and authority. That is a lie, or at least, an outdated concept. We don't need to wait for someone to give us permission.

The problem is also that we don't understand the concept of power. We rely on an old way of thinking that was responsible for keeping others obeying while a few increased their control.

We also don't appreciate the amount of power we currently hold. Once we understand the potential we have, we open a door to literally doing what others considered to be impossible.

Unfortunately, as well, we don't know how to leverage what we have into far more than we need.

So here we are, standing on the threshold of more opportunities than we can image but we are blind to the process. We could be and doing more, making more money, creating valuable products and services, while helping more people, but we don't think we have the power.

The Answer

To solve this problem, we need to pivot our understanding and approach to power. It isn't a scarce resource but a bountiful, renewable energy that is easily accessible. The answer to our problems come when we pivot from a mindset of poverty to one of affluence.

The answer is also found as we pivot our thinking and attitudes to embrace a growth mindset. Leave the fixed focus behind to open the door to leveraging our individual and collective power.

That will happen as we quit clinging to the past or the present and actively work to build a collaborative culture of success. This isn't a selfish grab for a scarce product as so many have claimed over the centuries. Power isn't there to grab but available for us to come together and leverage our collective power.

Once we make that shift, tremendous opportunities await.

Those that follow me know that I believe compassion is the pivotal component of the ultimate business success. To do what others never thought possible, we come alongside others to help alleviate their pain. It's all about helping others through whatever it is that distracts and prevents them from delivering their ultimate performance. Pain is traumatic but also subtle, hidden in the daily grind of frustrations. Helping to alleviate those frustrations allows them to thrive instead of simply struggling to survive. In business, that's when we see their performance increase as well as the department's production and the organizational profits. Success, personal or professional, is essentially helping others, team members, customers, and client's get what they want and need. In the end, we create opportunities when we notice, feel, and strategize how to help alleviate another's pain.

The answer is also making a pivotal shift from the outside-in thinking world that believes it is right side up when it is actually upside down. Outside-in thinking creates two crippling problems. First, it requires that we listen to an outsider who tells us what to do. We willingly relinquish our power to someone who doesn't care about our purpose or passion yet expect obedience.

Second, outside-in living prioritizes popularity over principle and purpose. Notice the innovators such as Elon Musk or Steve Jobs leverage their power by making the choice to defy convention. By going against popular opinion, they willingly violate best practices to do what others considered "impossible." Henry Ford famously said that if he would've asked his clients what they wanted, they would've said a faster horse. Albert Einstein's theory of relativity breaks the rules of Newton who was the best thinking of the day. Breakthroughs often require re-engineering our thinking, shifting perspectives, pivoting our paradigms, to see the answers to persistent problems. Popular thinking, i.e., living outside-in usually prevents pivotal thinking. Learning to live inside-out is the answer.

The Challenge

As an individual, your challenge is to lead your life and do what you ultimately imagine possible. Unfortunately, many have quit dreaming. They settled for ordinary because the ultimate seemed impossible. The challenge is to begin dreaming and believing again.

Do you believe your dreams could come true? Or have you become skeptical or maybe even cynical, doubting you can do what you consider impossible?

Your challenge may be to pivot from doubting to daring to believe.

Then your challenge may be that you need to willing to pivot from where you are to where you ultimately want to be. Some are pivoting from struggle to success while others are pivoting from ordinary to the ultimate. Many are pivoting from reactive to proactive, from the bleeding edge to the cutting edge. Every leader following the Covid pandemic and during a recession is pivoting from the old normal to the new normal.

As an individual, you are leading your own life, making your own choices. That means not "taking what the world gives" but making hard choices to get what you ultimately want. You are living your life instead of allowing others to dictate your destiny. To live inside-out in and outside-in world demands a powerful sense of passion and determination. There will be many that will attempt to deter you from your ultimate destination.

Pivoting is difficult and becoming pivotal is even tougher because it requires a sudden shift from what was predictable, safe, and comfortable. Difficult times are triggered by any trauma whether it be economic, pandemic, or environmental. Tough times can also be triggered by social unrest, technological develop, or other radical cultural changes. Together they create an immense challenge for organizational leaders in any space.

That is complicated by those attempting to lead with the old "Manifest Destiny" paradigm that fosters a "rape, pillage, and plunder because we can" mentality. Leaders are finding that approach antiquated, as reliable in our 2021 world as an analog cell phone. The downsizing of the 1980s left a disengaged workforce that shattered the world of employees at the time. Where once they could rely on predictable, lifetime employment, very quickly they had to pivot to the unwelcomed world of layoffs. In 2021 as we attempt to exit the pandemic, employers are trying to stem the turnover tsunami. The leadership challenge is to adjust to a new method of building and running an organization that stays abreast with the cutting-edge developments. Increasingly, that requires we think like an entrepreneur, not an employee.

Today world of business runs on a fast moving, entrepreneurial mindset, quickly and consistently pivoting to sense and seize the next, best opportunity. We can start businesses with only a phone, making money without a physical location or even employees. More and more are creating new technology or improving other technologies to offer products and services that quickly disrupt the market. Notice the industry leaders who profit without owning their own property (Zillow, Airbnb) or equipment (Lyft, Uber). Notice that an increasing number of employees are choosing to work the gig economy or create a startup on the side. The challenge as leaders inside and outside of the organization is to adapt to the new method of doing business.

In a world of the 24-hour news cycle, we can no longer hide our mistakes. We must be willing to be transparent and admit when we are wrong.

But even that is not news.

The leadership challenge is that we must pivot to the next normal. Today's consumer is driven by social and environmental sensitivity. Whether you agree or not, the perception of global warming is an issue that drives many of your customers either away or to your business. Your sensitivity to Black Lives Matter and LBGQTIA affects the very makeup of your organization. With an increasing sensitivity, organizations won't be able to keep the glass ceiling from shattering. The only choice leaders have is to pivot to the next, new normal.

As businesses rebuild following the pandemic in the summer of 2021, many are faced with a pivot they didn't see coming before March of 2020. Do they return everyone to the physical office as was their practice? Or do they pivot 180 degrees to an entirely virtual organization, reducing their financial costs. Or do they only pivot 90 degrees, creating a hybrid organization that is more flexible yet appreciating the value of physical proximity?

Notice how the pandemic unleashed potential that many leaders doubted and some still dismiss. Many employees were still productive despite working virtually. Without the grind of a commute, many found more time and money. It was as if they received a pay raise. My wife instantly gained 3 hours in her day and enjoyed having more money at the end of the month. But the benefits extended into her productivity. She was like many who appreciated the opportunity to work with fewer interruptions. Ignored projects received more attention. Imagine the challenge of leaving that productivity behind to reenter the office.

The downside to working from home or other locations takes two distinct directions. First, some employees shut down and took an exceptionally long vacation. Out of sight meant they could binge watch movies, attend to family issues or even take a part time job. Some even moved to a less expensive or more attractive location. In many ways, the pivot meant disengagement emotionally or physically. For the others, they became workaholics. Their work-life balance flew out of whack in part because of manager's violation of their private time. After all, they reasoned, I can reach them at any time. They no longer had the physical office presence as a barrier. For many, they can't wait to return to the office to limit their hours.

But that is only one side of the pivoting challenge. Organizations need synergy caused by spontaneous interactions. The unplanned meeting may trigger either a forgotten issue or create a new idea. For those seeking to progress up the ladder, visibility is critical to building credibility and likeability. Zoom or telephone calls sufficed but are not preferable.

Hidden in the pivot to the entirely virtual or hybrid organization is the opportunity to expand a limited workforce. Maybe this is the opportunity to create a diverse, global perspective. It may also be an opportunity to reduce your office costs and hire less expensive workers because they live in a more affordable location. That is a mindset pivot that some leaders are finding extremely difficult, but others are welcoming. The challenge is to figure out how to manage remote workers.

Then there is the issue of productivity and how to measure it. Maybe this is the time to pivot from paying people for time and start paying them for productivity. Those that struggled most with productivity based their thinking on a "butts in seats" mindset. Even though an employee watched movies, did crossword puzzles, or simply slacked off, as long as they were at their workstation, the leader could tolerate it. Often, they explained, "We don't have a way to measure their productivity." Interesting. In a world of gig workers paid for performance, why can't we find a way to measure it? The challenge is to pivot our thinking and measure productivity.

The Ultimate Challenge

Now for the ultimate challenge. We must become pivotal, not just adapt to one external event. The world is changing so rapidly and radically that we can expect continual, comprehensive, disruption that demands a drastically different mindset, perspective, and behavior.

How we led fifty years ago is no longer relevant. That is gone and we can't go back. Workers and customers think, feel, and behave with different expectations. Technology and globalization have shrunk the globe, connecting diverse people for a common goal. The harsh truth is that we are not returning to the old way of thinking. Gone are the days of slow, stable growth. Just look at the list of current, business leaders. The names of Facebook, Amazon, and Alibaba were not known until the last 3 or 4 decades. Notice the list of new billionaires and their ages. It isn't just older, white men who lead. The face of leaders has literally and figuratively changed.

Leadership Secrets

The not-so-well-kept secret is that our approach to leading ourselves, leading others, making money, and making a difference must change. Anyone can become a leader. Anyone can grow a business to become a millionaire or billionaire in just a few years. It isn't the privilege of the rich or the socially elite. People from around the globe and from any walk of life now have the power to do what most around them thought was impossible.

One of the secrets is that leadership is a proactive choice, not a reactive behavior. The world is changing too much and too fast to react to trends. Instead, we must become individuals and organizations that learn to anticipate the opportunities and the obstacles. Even though many organizations enjoy stability and leaders value control, the new normal is filled with unpredictability. Attempts to control are frustrated in an unpredictable world. Instead, leaders are wise to pivot by planning as much as possible, tracking the trends and anticipating the opportunities.

Another secret is that pivotal leaders think bigger and reach higher. We now have that opportunity to sense and seize the best opportunity, becoming the industry leader, unleashing the ultimate performance, production, and profits. Any leader has the opportunity to build a team that can pivot the organization to the new normal.

At the same time, we have recently seen that we can pivot from perfection to not-quite-finished. Microsoft has made billions by releasing less than perfect software. Open-source software developers capitalize on allowing others to help them build their idea. That is no longer a well-kept secret but too many don't leverage that knowledge.

The current world demands leaders become pivotal, continually monitoring the trends, and pursuing the best opportunities. That is a mindset and a practice. To pivot into that new normal requires exposing a leadership secret. That is another part of a poorly kept secret but one too many leaders have purposely ignored it. For years we have heard that the best way to lead is to build a power base upon networks of influential people in important positions.

That sounds reasonable, doesn't it?

As I've studied leadership, business success and disruptive innovation over the last four decades, that did indeed seem to be the best method for those days.

But maybe we missed something.

> *"As we look ahead into the next century, leaders will be those who empower others."*
> Bill Gates

Bill Gates and other leaders who follow this mindset turn convention on its head. Empowering others is the secret to leading in the future. The one who celebrates their team engages them and strengths not just the employee but the team. Instead of a self-centered hoarding of power, the leader leverages rather than wields power. That is the secret to creating a flexible and successful organization that overcomes the largest of obstacles and emerge from the pack. The secret to pivoting is leveraging power.

The Dirty Little Secret

As I mentioned, this is a poorly kept but often ignored secret. Recently I heard a leader proclaim, "we hire talented people and then never let them reach their potential." Why would anyone do that? That only serves the ego of a misguided individual thinking they are wielding power.

They can't see how hiring talented people and letting them do what they do best is actually increasing their power. They ignore that the way to increase power is to leverage it, not wield it. They need to pivot from controlling people to building influence. They increase their influence by building their reputation, increasing their authority, unleashing their ability, and tapping their energy. The dirty little secret is that the ego of an insecure leader stymies the most talented individuals and teams. Too many leaders give lip service to engagement, collaboration, and empowerment but resist any action that doesn't make them look good. They hesitate to develop their team lest they get promoted. Too often they fear a zero-sum game where they are left behind.

The dirty little secret is that too many stay in those demeaning environments when they could be starting their own side hustle that could be their ticket out. They doubt themselves for the very reason that insecure leader never developed them. They don't develop because the leader wants to control them. We sacrifice our power, willingly setting it aside for a secure paycheck that diminishes our potential.

That dirty little secret shows a small, minded individual who doesn't appreciate their unique value and hidden power. They compete instead of collaborating, wielding whatever power they perceive in an effort to claim their authority. That dirty little secret is costing individuals and the organization by remaining ridged when the opportunity demands flexibility. We don't unleash our ultimate because we work in a place that doesn't see it, won't appreciate it, and are afraid of the results when we achieve it. We don't leverage our power because we allow someone else to limit it.

Imagine what happens when we realize the potential we have. Imagine how our lives will change for the better when we learn to leverage our power by re-engineering our thinking, harnessing our emotions, and strategically reaching higher. Notice how much more we will be able to do by pivoting our perspective to opportunities instead of obstacles. Then notice how our world begins to pivot to what we ultimately want when we collaborate with like-minded people instead of competing for scarce rewards.

"Talent wins games, but teamwork and intelligence win championships."
Michael Jordan

The Unique Value of this Book

This book provides a value that no other book does. You will gain an understanding about power not described anywhere else. Here you will find my thoughts on the four elements of compassion power. My insight is the result of the process you have just read. My pivot began as I left warehouse work to return to college, finishing the final 3 years of my undergraduate degree in communication studies. Continuing in my graduate studies and research, I focused on the power of language to create and destroy. I learned to dissect language to unleash its hidden power. By putting the concept of power under the microscope, I reveal insights that others overlook.

I will remind you of the obvious but also reveal some aspects of pivotal leadership that should be obvious, but they are not. Some secrets are poorly kept but when we hear them, we say, "I knew that." noticing the obvious and hidden is part of my role as an executive coach, author, and consultant.

This book is unique in that I discuss power within the framework of compassion. Too many business leaders consider compassion as an unwise expense. However, in my work, I've found compassion to be the key to employee engagement and, therefore, the critical component to pivotal leadership and innovation. To lead from the cutting edge and to emerge as an industry leader, we are wise to build teams that come alongside and help others alleviate their pain. This applies to peers, managers, executives, subordinates, customers, vendors, and the general public. In the *Pivotal Compassion* and *Pivotal Engagement* books, my coauthor (my wife who works in Human Resources) detail how the theoretical and tactical components of compassion foster the ultimate performance, production, and profit in the workplace.

Another unique value of this book is my perspective. I've worked warehouse and factory jobs as a floor worker. Notice what it took to make that pivot. I went from punching a time clock and receiving a weekly check to creating my own livelihood. Also notice the pivot from employee to leader, teaching undergraduates and graduates. Within that pivot, notice that may violate your own perception of a leader. Too many don't see teaching in a classroom as leading. They see it as dispensing information or babysitting.

I've not only studied leadership but also worked with returning adult students actively serving as leaders in small, medium, and large organizations in for profit and nonprofit. They represented military, government, and religious organizations domestically and internationally. I've also led as a college professor, department chair, executive coach, mastermind facilitator, and podcast how where I interviewed leaders.

This book is powerful because it also reveals a secret I have learned and applied. Since September of 2007, I have written approximately 29 books. I will write at least another 5 in the next six months. How do I do that? I tap my energy, hone my abilities, claim my authority to increase my influence. In other words, I leverage my power to do the impossible.

My unique value comes from a balance between experience and observation. There is tremendous value in personal experience. You have lived it. Many who coach and consult from personal experience provide valuable insights. However, there is a tendency to use past experience as a proven formula for future action. Pivotal leaders recognize that in a radically and rapidly changing world, what worked yesterday may not work today or tomorrow. That's where observation plays an essential role.

Observation through watching, reading, and researching provides aa perspective that personal experience cannot. Balancing the two into one perspective provides a unique inside-out and outside-in view that provides the best of both worlds.

Preview

In this short book, you will read about becoming pivotal before learning about definitions of power. You will be confronted with the 12 limitations of traditional power. From there we discuss the concept of compassion before moving into the four aspects of compassion power. By reading this book you will build a foundation for engaging employees to build your pivotal success. The checklists are provided both as a review and a guide to implementing the information. For the tactical application of this material, check out *Pivotal Engagement* and *Pivotal Compassion*.

Loren Murfield, Ph.D.

PIVOTAL OPPORTUNITIES

Pivotal opportunities emerge every day when we are willing to make the choice to change.
Loren Murfield

To sense and then seize the next, great opportunities, we need to do what we never imagined was possible. We must pivot from who we are to who we are willing to become so we can do what needs to be done. Seizing those pivotal opportunities requires every ounce of power you currently possess. It will take leveraging that power to increase your energy, ability, authority, and influence.

My Story

My story is a prime example of becoming pivotal against one's will. It wasn't that I grew up like Richard Branson with an entrepreneurial mindset. It was exactly the opposite. As I explain in my autobiographical *Pitchfork to Ph.D.*, I was a chore boy follower. I did what I was told and trembled at the thought of getting in trouble. I followed the rules and adopted the mindset of an obedient worker.

While I was one of the best order fillers in our section of the warehouse, I wasn't management material. I didn't want to lead, in part, because I was too insecure. I was also too wedded to a strict set of values that often-criticized management. No wonder I couldn't see opportunities to move up. I was wasting my energy on what I couldn't change.

Part of that insecurity was being married to someone equally as insecure and even more caustic. By the time the ten-year marriage ended, I had no self-esteem left. I hated my life because I didn't see any opportunities.

I had dreams but didn't believe I had the power to make any difference. On occasion, I had hopes when a few opportunities appeared.

We become pivotal by developing the habit of sensing and seizing the best opportunities. That requires constantly making ourselves notice to become aware of what is available and how we can get to it. Anything less will leave us struggling to survive in a rapidly and rapidly changing world when others are thriving.

For me that came in volunteering to preach in the church where I grew up. Volunteering is simply making ourselves available. Speaking in public isn't a task that many want to do, especially in a small, remote farming community. In volunteering, I leveraged my earlier study of the bible that very few had. Soon, pastors were calling me to fill in so they could go on vacation.

The best opportunities require more than merely following best practices, getting a job, obeying a boss, following a lock step program. Instead, a radical new way of thinking is needed. To think bigger, we need to move from where we have been most comfortable to see trends from a new, refreshing angle. Then we will develop an audacious attitude that gladly welcomes cutting edge knowledge and broadening of our skills.

Feeling safe, preaching to my home congregation filled with neighbors, friends, and family, I saw the opportunity to improve upon the stoic, dry sermons. I creatively pivoted to using metaphors that they could relate to. One Sunday I preached in bib overalls like most of the men wore during the week. Another day I preached using an dry branch from the trees on the farm. Then there was preaching on harvesting during the time farmers were combining their oats. My dad, who rarely commented on the sermon, told me he liked the one about the eagle the best.

As more opportunities grew, so did my confidence and my willingness to look for more opportunities.

That pivot created a new approach to life and work, gladly developing habitual change. In a tiny way, I was beginning to break free of my fixed mindset. I ever so slightly cracked open a change mindset. I slowly began to let go of old habits, even though they were unproductive. I slowly began to pivot to see a world filled with opportunities.

But my pivot out of warehousing wasn't entirely my choice. Even though I knew there was something better, I needed a stable job with a wife and three kids. It was only in my attempt to hold the family together when threatened with divorce that I left the job hoping for a different manual labor job. Eventually she separated and took the kids. In the process, she went enrolled in college, something I had wanted for many years.

That is when I made my choice to pivot. In some ways, it was an easy choice because I had nothing left. No money. No marriage. No job. When you are lying flat on your back, the only way you can look is up.

I also didn't think I had any power. Returning to college as a noncustodial father just prior to my 31st birthday left me feeling like an oddball. I didn't drink so my social life was limited to the church. But being single at 31 is too old for the college group and they had no singles ministry. I didn't have the power of many friendships. Remember, I also didn't have any confidence.

Then there was going back to school to study subjects like math that I hadn't tackled since my freshman year in high school. My biology lab was especially troublesome. I flunked the first exam because I had absolutely no clue. I felt powerless. My saving grace was being so desperate that I asked the guy across the lab table for help. That saved me as I struggled to get through with the course with a "C." From there I saw the opportunity to make better choices. It turned out I had other choices for to fulfil my lab requirements and pursued them.

Notice the power of asking for help. Opportunities emerge when we let go of our ego. For me it helped that I felt so worthless that I didn't have anything to protect.

That one moment of asking for help pivoted my world, even though I didn't fully realize it. I had been obeying for so long I didn't know how to make good decisions and was too timid to ask for help.

Part of my upbringing believed that being a good leader didn't ask for help. They learned to tough it out and do it on their own. When I was willing to let go of that misperception, I began to see opportunities.

I didn't realize it during that time, but it wasn't only my world that was changing constantly and with increasing speed. Even in this small college town in the middle of the country, change happened, even though they worked to limit change. With that decision to ask for help, I also had the courage to ask for more information.

American History quickly became my favorite course, and I was contemplating declaring it as my major and going on to teach college. Prior to class one day, I mentioned to my professor, Dr. Sweeney, that I was enjoying the course so much I was considering declaring history my major. He surprised me when he said, "I wouldn't advise it. There are no jobs at this time." Once again, there is power in asking and listening.

I learned this lesson again at the end of the semester. Anxious to learn how well I did that first semester, I stopped at Dr. Sweeny's office. My grade was slightly below an A and not quite close enough to justify his bumping it up. Without ever asking, because I had been in class, sat up front, and engaged him, he voluntarily pivoted it from a "B" to an "A." Little did he or I know at that moment, but that allowed me to make Dean's list for my first semester. From there, I had the confidence to strive for a perfect 4.0 average each semester. Even though I never quite achieved it, I earned grades to qualify for graduate studies.

Notice the opportunities that emerged even though I was at one of the worst times of my life. Instead of flunking biology, I asked for help. Instead of declaring a major, I engaged a professor in the field. Instead of sitting back and waiting for a grade, I went to his office and asked.

Each of those situations were opportunities to ask and listen. Pivoting from those old habits of self-sufficiency that weren't working for me, opened up my ultimate opportunity to teach college with a Ph.D. That opportunity opened up an entirely new world that I had never imagined, becoming an executive coach, author, consultant, and entrepreneur.

Notice that my life is a story of becoming pivotal. I never thought I could do anything significant but leveraged what little power I had to do what I never imagined. Remember, I was the chore boy of the family. I shoveled so much cow, pig, and chicken manure that I felt like a piece of it. Many thought my dreams were impossible.

Pivotal opportunities emerge every day when we are willing to make the choice to change. With that habit of continual change, we leverage our power as we become pivotal. That is the key. We gain more power to seize our ultimate opportunity as we develop the attitude, knowledge, skills, and set our goal to continually shift our perspective.

The flip side of becoming pivotal is the challenge. Seizing our next, great opportunity will demand everything we have and much more. Einstein famously said that we cannot solve our problems with the same thinking we used to create them. In the same way, doing what we never thought possible will require that we see the world differently, acquire new knowledge, think much bigger, and hone new skills. We cannot do what we never thought possible when we continue to think the same old way. We need to empower our pivotal thinking.

One of the ways we do that is to shift paradigms. We change the way we see the world and how it works. That includes how we understand the concept of power.

Checklist: Pivotal Opportunities

- ☐ What opportunities do you see?
- ☐ How will changing your attitude help?
- ☐ How can you develop the powerful habit and reputation of being pivotal?
- ☐ How will these opportunities pivot you toward your ultimate success?

Pivotal Power

PIVOTAL CHOICES

Realizing you have a choice gives you power.
Loren Murfield

I have great news for you. If I can do it, so can you. You learned by reading my story that I didn't get to this point by being extremely talented or from my wealthy and influential parents. It all came down to making a pivotal choice to do what you and others never thought possible.

My Choices
Remember in that first semester back in college where I decided to become a college professor. I had been doing some preaching and enjoyed helping others. Then as I went back to college, I started noticing more about what it took. The first thing I noticed was that it required a Ph.D. or other doctorate. As I declared a major of communication studies, I looked farther. I would need to graduate with honors from my bachelor's program to be admitted into a master's program. There I had to not only complete the typical 2-year program but earn good grades. Then I had to complete an original research project they called a thesis. From there I needed to be accepted into a Ph.D. program where I faced two years of study followed by written comprehensive exams and completing another original research project called the dissertation.

Notice the many choices required to teach college. In the same way, choosing to become a pivotal leader and do things that you and others never imagined, is your choice. It doesn't matter where you were born or to what parents. Becoming pivotal doesn't depend on economics or ethnicity. It's not dictated by anyone or anything except you. To sense and seize the next, great opportunities depends on the choices you make.

Realizing our Choices

We all have choices. Unfortunately, sometimes we don't realize it. We do what we think we have to do because we can't see any other way. Vitor Frankl survived German concentration camps during World War II in part because he understood he had a choice. He could choose to shape his own perspective. Just recognizing that he had that choice was what made the difference in his survival. He realized that even though he was a prisoner, he chose his own destiny.

"The camp inmate was frightened of making decisions and of taking any sort of initiative whatsoever. This was the result of a strong feeling that fate was one's master, and that one must not try to influence it in any way, but instead let it take its own course."
Viktor E. Frankl, "Man's Search for Meaning."

Realize is defined as
- "to grasp or understand clearly.
- to make real; give reality to (a hope, fear, plan, etc.).
- to bring vividly to the mind.
- to convert into cash or money:"

(www.Dictionary.com)

Realizing is noticing what others didn't and then cashing in on the opportunity to choose. It is clearly understanding and appreciating what can happen. That perspective changes seemingly hopeless situations.

Think about what Frankl went through. He faced death every day from 1942 to 1945. It all started when he was practicing medicine as a psychologist. He was wrongfully imprisoned simply because of his

Jewish ethnicity. He was moved across four concentration camps, including Auschwitz where his brother died and his mother was killed. Auschwitz, the very name still reeks of fear, the place where over one million people were gassed to death by the Nazis. Imagine facing death and recognizing you have a choice.

In many ways, he had a right to be angry and bitter. The circumstances entitled him to an emotional reaction. Instead, he chose to think logically. He recognized he had a choice and that was what gave him the power to survive when others gave up and died. (www.goodtherapy.org)

Frankl says that even when suffering is unavoidable, we can find meaning, and therefore, opportunity. If "one cannot change a situation that causes his suffering, he can still choose his attitude."

Your Challenge
- Stop and notice.
- What choices do you have that you didn't realize?

Choose Your Position

We choose our attitude. Meriam-Webster defines attitude as a mental position or an emotion about someone or something. That definition shows us that attitude is based on our perspective.

Frankl looked at suffering different than most in the concentration camps. Instead of seeing suffering as inevitable and hopeless, he shifted to see the best in the worst situations. That shift in perspective, purposely taking a different position helps pivot from suffering to achievement and accomplishment. It also helps us make ourselves better and take significant actions.

Imagine being sent to a prison where you know one million people like yourself have been murdered. Now imagine shifting your attitude to see how you can make a difference to those around you. It's as if you were looking at an object on the table and walked to the other side to see it in a different light. Notice how that give you hope and power. Suddenly, with a different view, you see opportunities.

Attitudes come from our beliefs and values. Beliefs are what we hold to be true while values are the priorities we set. For example, I believe that everyone has choices and that taking away one's choice is wrong. (Beliefs) Meanwhile, I value my freedom to do what I think is best. I also value making the world a better place. In addition, I value personal responsibility. (Values) Therefore, I have a low opinion of those who demand someone obey simply to foster their insecurities. (Attitude).

Realizing you have a choice gives you power. Too often people lead their lives in obedience to others. They feel imprisoned to a job, career, or relationship. They don't see their power to learn new skills, pursue an education, or seek a promotion. They don't think they have options when it comes to their family or friends. Sadly, because they can't see the choice, they won't take the necessary action because they don't believe they have the power. Unfortunately, many stay in abusive relationships because they don't think they have the power to escape their abuser.

Others are imprisoned to powers within themselves. They don't think they have a choice to let go of past grievances and forgive. They don't see how they can escape their personality quirks or character flaws. The future is fixed because they don't think they have a choice to change who they are. "That's not who I am" they argue. Sadly, they don't see the choice is theirs to change.

Still others are addicted to drugs, sex, money, or attention. They live on the emotional high from something they don't believe they can live without. At first, they don't see a problem. Then, when the addiction starts to overtake their life, they deny there is a problem. Finally, when they hit bottom, they either self-destruct or ask for help. Notice the inability to see their choices and the future based on those choices.

Notice how we build up walls in our minds that put us in a concentration camp. It's not just a prison with impenetrable walls. This is worse because we beat ourselves and others who think they have a choice. We are so trained to obey that we wouldn't walk out the gate if it were flung wide open. Instead, we convince ourselves that the limited opportunities are safer. Even when someone tells them there is a buffet waiting outside the gates, they doubt they should go. They list a number of reasons, but all are transparent to those who are enjoying the feast.

Sometimes they, actually we, lie to ourselves claiming that we are helping others like us, and it is better to stay where we are. After all, lottery winners claim the money won't change them. We say we don't want to be rich because "money is the root of all evil." Never mind that the good book is misquoted. It is the love of money, unbridled greed, that is the root of all evil. We convince ourselves of an ordinary destiny because that is what is best. In reality, we don't want or think we deserve that change. Even more, we can't see life beyond that breakthrough. In our ordinary thinking, we gladly forfeit any opportunity we fear will change who we are.

Breaking through that barrier will take considerable power. But rest assured, there is power in becoming more than we are right now.

Unfortunately, many times we live with the scarcity because we are afraid to fail. In our mind, we rationalize turning down incredible opportunities because failure is the ultimate embarrassment. That poverty thinking tells us to pinch that penny tightly as there won't be another for a while. Instead, a pivotal thinker tracks the trends and forecasts the opportunities to minimize the risk and maximize the success. Shifting that paradigm does require a powerful desire and diligent work.

Your Life = Your Choice

Understand this very basic idea. You control your own destiny by the choices you make. If you choose to succeed, you will. Please understand that to choose doesn't mean simply saying you want it. Choosing means committing to the shift, putting it as your top priority, and then relentlessly pursuing it until your dream is a reality. Choosing is a commitment, not a wish or wimpy promise.

The question is, are you willing to choose? At this point, don't worry about failing or not maintaining your commitment. Right now, focus on your willingness to choose what you want. It isn't up to anyone else. It is up to you.

The commitment comes each day as you once again decide. You see, making a choice is a daily, actually a constant, minute by minute decision. You will be tempted with lesser options, but you choose to maintain your quest of the ultimate. There is power in each one of those small choices. There is even more power in that string of small choices.

Notice there is no middle ground. There is no, "Yes, but . . ." answer. Notice also there is no explaining when someone uses the phrase, "You need to understand. . ." No, choosing is an either-or choice. Once you choose "Yes," you have empowered yourself to say yes again and again. Claim your power to choose to do the impossible.

Checklist: Power in Choosing

It takes power to choose yet knowing you have a choice gives you power. Exercise your power to make a change in your life by making the following choices.

Thinking
Do you choose to think bigger?
- ☐ Yes
- ☐ No

Do you choose to think beyond your doubts?
- ☐ Yes
- ☐ No

Reaching
Do you choose to reach higher?
- ☐ Yes
- ☐ No

Doing
Do you choose to do what you never thought possible?
- ☐ Yes
- ☐ No

Being
Do you choose to become pivotal?
- ☐ Yes
- ☐ No

DEFINING POWER

> *"Every human has four endowments - self-awareness, conscience, independent will and creative imagination. These give us the ultimate human freedom... The power to choose, to respond, to change."*
> Stephen Covey

Power is an interesting concept. We all use the term but, if pressed, have difficulty defining it. We have to stop and think, and even then, often stumble for a concise definition.

Let's try it. "What is your definition of power?"

Stop. Do not read any further until you answer it. You can even say the answer out loud or write it down.

Once you have your answer, we can move on.

It is important that you come to your definition before we delve deep into a series of questions and answers that will likely alter your perspective of power.

Are you ready? Let's begin.

What is Power?

We define power as "the ability to sense and seize our best opportunities." This definition is derived from Rollo May's classic "Power and Innocence" (1972) where he defines power as 'the ability to cause or prevent change." (p. 100). This concise definition is attractive as it has the integrity of the term's origins. However, to deliver disruptive innovation, we want to focus on the positive change. As we will see in the following pages, change can be productive or destructive; we each have the power to make things better or worse.

But as compassionate and effective leaders, we want to focus on the productive change. Therefore, we limit our definition of power to the positive.

Why are Word Origins Important?

Words are far more than mere labels we use to transfer knowledge. Instead, words and gestures are symbols that we use to negotiate a shared meaning with one or more people. Words are the things we use to create meaning. We use words to communicate by talking and listening, reading, and writing words. Words give us the power to communicate by creating the message we want to share. Without words, we lack power to create.

Despite the misperception, words are not simple. Words have a dictionary meaning but also a common meaning. Sometimes we have several words for the same thing like rocket, grinder, hoagie or sub, all are the same type of sandwich. The words "pop" and "soda" refer to the same thing, but like the sandwich, vary depending on geography. Go into the Deep South and order a "Coke" and they may ask you "What kind? We have Pepsi, Coke, 7UP and Root Beer." All are soft drinks but with different words representing them. One thing might have several different words to describe it.

But the opposite is also true; we may have one word that refers to many different things and have several different meanings. "Home" can be where we are currently living or where we grew up. Telling someone we are "going home" might lead to a variety of assumptions. Are we going to our current residence? To our childhood home? Or somewhere else?

Knowing how the other person is using a word at that time gives us power to understand them and the situation better. We care when we take the time to consider how the other person is using the word. We communicate when we care enough to work together to create shared meaning.

"How do Words Change?"

Words are dynamic, always changing because culture, civilization and daily life is forever evolving. Technology is helping to change the world at an increasingly rapid pace. More and more we are being connected with people, places, and ideas for the first time. So we mix those into our lives and need words to express what that means to us. Therefore, language has to change, it has to evolve. What it meant a decade ago, it may not mean today. That is why we look back to see where and how the word originated to better understand the term we are using and then to understand how it is used in the world around us.

What is Confusing about Power?

The word "power" is often considered to be interchangeable with influence, control, energy and even authority. Although there is overlap in these terms, there is a significant difference and that creates the confusion. By narrowly defining them, we will be better able to understand the concepts and leverage our power more effectively. In the end, we want to leverage our power to do what naysayers and followers think is impossible. That means we will maximize our energy, increase our authority and elevate our influence.

Power is the *Ability* to sense and seize the best opportunities. The critical element is "the ability to" do what you ultimately find most beneficial. Without that ability, nothing else matters. That is why power is so critically important to success. That is also why no one can empower us. We will discuss that later in the book.

Authority is the power given to a person due to their position in an organization. One has authority if they have the power to accept or reject, to reward or punish. Without that position power, they have no authority. Power is the *ability* and authority is the *permission* to use that ability.

Influence is the method to get the results of the ability and authority. We influence others when we exercise our authority and use our ability to get the desired result. That means power is the ability, authority is the permission and influence is the result.

Energy is the driving force that makes the ability possible. We have no ability if we no strength, intensity, or motivation to take the action. But when we have that energy and enough of that energy, we then have the ability to take the action.

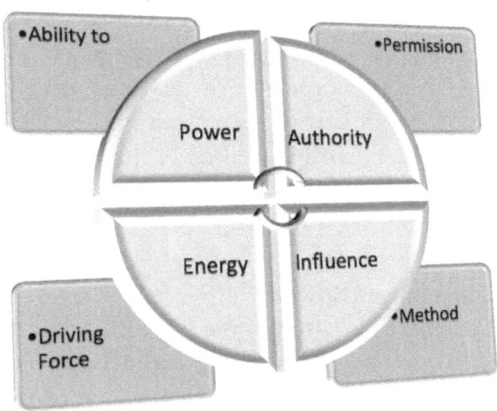

What does it mean to be Powerless?

Being powerless is having no power to make the positive changes we desire. We have no ability to sense our opportunities. We do not know that they exist and cannot see them. If we do, we have no clue which ones are realistic and which ones are mirages. Furthermore, we are powerless when we have no ability to seize those opportunities we do see. Like a person in prison looking out, we have no ability to make our dreams happen. We lack the process, resources, or motivation to make it happen.

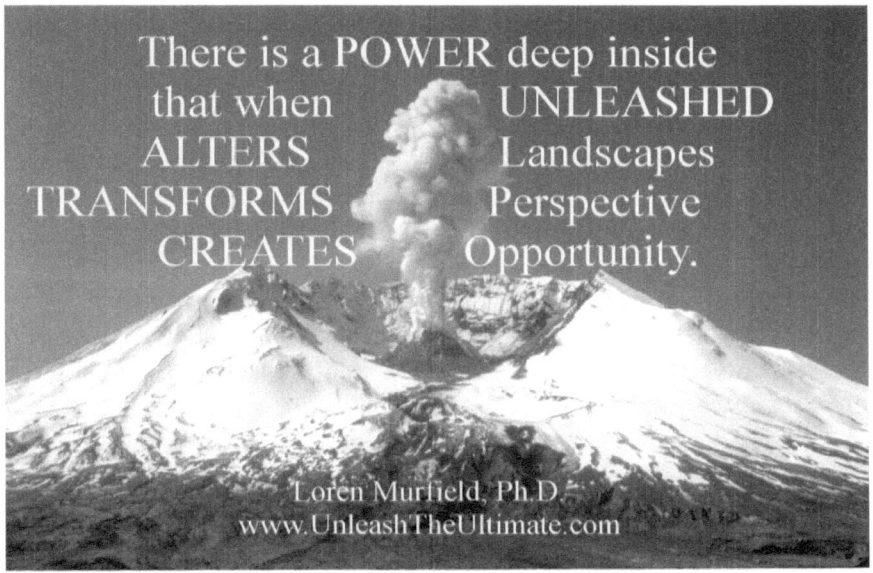

Who has Power?

Everyone has power and everyone has more power than they realize. At this very minute when you are reading this, there are more opportunities available to you than you can ever seize. Never before in the history of the world has an individual had more opportunity than we do today. We have more ability to communicate via mobile devices that can connect us to almost anywhere in the world. We have more ability to collaborate with others, build a following, sell a product, offer a service, fund a cause, or create some sort of revolutionary transformation. As an individual, we have never had this much opportunity before.

The availability of those opportunities is power in itself. Most do not realize this. Some do not know about these opportunities, so they never use that power. They are blind to what they are able to do. Sometimes we are blind simply because we didn't open our eyes or focus on the right place.

Others believe they are powerless because they do not have the process. They can see the opportunity but cannot see how they can make it happen. Meanwhile, scores of videos sit on YouTube or other internet sites waiting to be played. Each of these two has a latent power waiting to be engaged. They need a leader to show them the key they already have tucked away in their pocket.

Still others are powerless due to their own insecurities, doubting that they can make the difference. They discredit the power they do have, often measuring it against the power they perceive others to have. They let the opportunities slip through their fingers because they doubted their grip was sufficient. Doubt is a disempowering disease that saps the energy from our mental, physical, and economical muscles. But amazingly, once we begin believing in ourselves, we begin to seize the power and do things we thought was impossible. Oddly enough, once we have done it, we often look back and say, "That wasn't nearly as difficult as I thought."

Power is the "ability to sense and seize opportunities."

Unfortunately, there are also those that are crippled by their cynicism. They believe change is harmful or that the results are not worth pursuing. Those individuals forfeit their power in favor of their own secured world of limited beliefs. The latter are indeed powerless to change unless they change their perspective and attitude. Even though the power is available their mindset prevents using it. The limitations become a self-imposed prison. When anyone moves beyond that limited mindset, they find more power than they imagined.

Can Power be Given?

Power is the "ability to sense and seize opportunities." That ability can be developed but never given. To have power is to not only have the ability to sense and seize our best opportunities but to do it. There is a distinct different between potential and actualizing that ability. There is a significant difference between having an opportunity and seizing it. In other words, we must take the action to have the power. We must overcome the obstacle to have the success. That means that power is active not passive.

May (1972) contends that "power cannot, strictly speaking, be given to another, for then the recipient still owes it to the giver. It must in some sense be assumed, taken, asserted. For unless it can be held against opposition, it is not power and will never be experienced as real on the part of the recipient." (p. 145).

We do not have any power if we rely on someone to give us the ability. We realize our power when we do something that gets the desired result.

We do not have any power if we rely on someone to give us the ability. We realize our power when we do something that gets the desired result.

For example, each of us has far more power when we get a job and earn the money to buy our first car instead of someone giving us the money for the car. We have more power because we are not relying on anyone else. We have earned the job and the money and therefore, have the funds to make the choice. As long as we are employed and maintain good credit, we maintain that power to purchase another car. If someone gives us a car or the money, we have that power only as long as they continue providing. Apart from them, we have no power. However, while we remain employable, we maintain the power to purchase on our own.

We realize this is splitting hairs but want to make a point. We have power when we earn the right to make decisions. We do not really have much power when the right to choose can be taken away.

For example, spoiled kids who never had to work for anything but were always given what they wanted or needed think they have a lot of power. However, when the difficulties arise, they are often powerless to resolve the situation without dad's or mom's power. Meanwhile, those who are challenged and develop their ability will discover their power that endures.

I agree with May that power cannot be given. This is why I avoid using the word "empower" because it has a sense that one can give power to another. We don't look for someone to give us power, but rather to learn how to make great choices that generate the power we need. We need to reposition our perspective, change our beliefs and reprioritize our values to develop our abilities to sense and seize the best opportunities. When we do that, we have leveraged an incredible opportunity to do what others never thought possible.

Is there Freedom without Power?

No. Freedom is the exemption from external control. We all desire the ability to do what we want at the time we desire. We all want as much control as we can handle. But we can never handle that control if we do not know how to sense which opportunities are the best or how to seize them. We can never be free if we do not have the power to realize those opportunities.

Look back and notice the opportunities you have missed. Very likely, you didn't have the ability to see your choice or how that opportunity could develop.

Why is Individual Power so Important Today?

Remember what we discussed in the introduction. Never before have we had so many opportunities at our fingertips. With the internet and social media, we have opportunities to be important. We can build a following in a relatively short amount of time. In that spotlight, we are important, at least to our followers. People have built their world on being important more than delivering value.

Notice how that same process can be used to foster entrepreneurial opportunities. Instead of working for a large corporation, we have choices to start our own business, earn our own income, choose where we want to live, and how we live our lives. Never before have we had these opportunities.

Each of us has the power to sense and seize our own best opportunities.

Is Power Limited?

No, power is not limited. It is a renewable energy that has unlimited potential.

In a personal setting, we often put limits our own power in a variety of ways. We claim, "I can't do that" or "This is impossible." We forfeit our opportunities with excuses such as "Dad would never allow that" or "I don't have the money, time or resources."

Does this seem possible to you?

The skeptic or the critic will say, "You can't do anything you want." I would agree that there are somethings that are not possible. I remember working with a former NFL player and dreaming that I was trying out for an NFL team. When I woke up, I had a good laugh because I was in my 50s and didn't have the body or the dexterity to play at that level.

But my point is that we have more power than we usually grasp and can do far more than we think possible. That is because power is not limited or hoarded. Instead, when we shift positions and see how power can be generated with synergy it becomes a renewable, not scarce, resource. We don't need to rely on someone else for the power they will give but rather utilize the abundance of power we can generate.

As we will discuss, power is energy. How much energy can you create? How much passion can you find? Look at the artists that have plugged into their art. Dolly Parton grew up in poverty in a Smokey Mountain hollow near Sevierville, Tennessee. But that didn't stop her. She went on to write 700 songs and sell over 100 million records. Is there a to her potential? She is still working feverishly as she approaches 80 years old.

Is power limited?

In some organizations, you won't be able to do what you want to do. In some situations, you will be stymied. However, when you collaborate with like-minded people, you will find more opportunities than you imagined. Life is not hopeless because one door closes because of an authority that doesn't see it your way. There are many other opportunities and probably many other ways to get what you ultimately want.

What does Power Look Like?

Power is actually invisible, but the process and the results can be seen easily. Power comes in many forms ranging from the subtle to the blatant. Joseph Nye, Jr. sees hard, soft, and smart power. (*The Future of Power,* 2011 and *The Powers to Lead,* 2008). "Hard power rests on inducements (carrots) and threats (sticks). But sometimes one can get the desired outcomes by setting the agenda and attracting others without threat or payment." Soft Power is "getting the outcomes one wants by attracting others rather than manipulating their material incentives. It co-opts people rather than coerces them. Soft power rests on the ability to shape the preferences of others to want what you want." (Nye, 2008, p. 29). Meanwhile, Smart Power is "the combination of the hard power of coercion and payment with the soft power of persuasion and attraction. (p. xiii).

Are there Levels of Power?

Yes. We have three main levels of power.

First, we have tactical power, the ability to take immediate action. No matter what level of a position we hold in an organization, no matter what economic level we enjoy, we always possess a power to act. We can choose to pursue certain opportunities to learn, plan, work and react. We have the power to be happy or sad, active, or passive, perfectionist or sloppy. We choose to do what we are assigned and what we do in our free time.

Second, we have operational power, the ability to set up processes and procedures that coordinate the tactical action.

Third, we have strategic power, the ability to envision what the world can be and how that world can operate.

What is the Difference Between Power and Force?
Many see a world with only a few, limited opportunities. Therefore, they do what they think they have to do, force their hand. They see a world of intense competition and survival of the fittest. To win in this world, they know they must work harder and demand the most from their team. If they don't succeed, they must try harder or push their team harder with rules, policy regulations, and swift punishment. They cannot afford to trust others. To ultimately succeed, they believe, they must *force* the situation.

At the same time, there are leaders who see a world filled with incredible opportunities. Their first challenge is to sense the best ones for them, their team, and their community. To seize the best opportunities, they leverage rather than wield power to build a cohesive team. For them, trust is a central component. No force is needed but rather constantly working to connect so they can collaborate and then create. Their focus is developing relationships instead of enforcing rules. With those relationships, each person willingly comes together to collaborate and create the solution to significant problems. Their ultimate success comes from leveraging the power to unleash the ultimate opportunities.

Power unleashes while forces restrict. Paraphrasing Hawkins (2002) in his classic *Power vs Force*, power energizes the world while force sucks the energy out of the room.

Why are We So Powerless to Control in the 3D World?

Many insist on holding onto the antiquated definition of power, "getting someone to do what we want them to do." The problem with this definition is that violates the norms of the Sharing Economy. Sharing operates on different foundational values that control. While sharing thrives on trust and collaboration, control is driven by fear. Sharing is open to a glut of opportunities where control narrows our choices often to "my way or the highway." They are powerless because they seek to control or force their success.

Why do People Fight for Power?

Too many believe power is limited and scarce so they fight for what they can get. No wonder they assume that they can and must hoard power like physical possessions. They believe they are fighting for authority and control because it is the only way to win in a competitive world. For them, power is the ability to survive. They don't see the difference between power and force. To succeed, they believe they have to force the situation and battle for authority to gain control. Once they have authority and control, they believe they can dictate their plan to others.

To do what you ultimately want to do, you need to pivot to a position where power is unlimited and yields more great opportunities than you can imagine.

Myths About Power

In our attempt to do exceed our expectations and those of others, we often view power as the force we possess to coerce others to give us what we want. That conflicts with our concept of pivotal power that merges ability, influence, authority, energy.

The old definition of power is a myth. The term, "myth" can be seen in two specific ways. First, myth is understood to be a lie or something false. Second, myth also refers to stories that make sense of our reality. Too many build their lives on the myth of power reflected in traditional thinking. I believe they are building their lives on lies because there is a better way. The traditional view of power isn't the best way to pursue our ultimate opportunities in this knowledge age

> *"The great enemy of the truth is very often not the lie, deliberate, contrived and dishonest, but the myth, persistent, persuasive and unrealistic."*
> John F. Kennedy

We generate the power to do the impossible when we see power as flexible, constant, multidimensional, and multifaceted.

Leveraging Power

Power is often thought of as wielding force. Instead, as we discussed in the types of power chapter, we pivot our power to do the impossible when we foster rapport and trust. We leverage results far bigger than the amount of effort usually expected.

Archimedes was the mathematician behind the lever. He is quoted as saying, "Give me a place to stand, and I can move the earth." He knew he and anyone who knew the principles behind leverage could do far more than they ever thought possible. Surely no one can lift the earth, but with enough leverage anything is possible. While we don't want to fixate on that extreme example, working with others, leveraging their energy, ability, and authority will allow us all to enjoy an influence far beyond what we could do were brute strength.

Synergy leverages power. Compassion leverages power. Teams leverage far more power than one a single individual can do. Rewarding often leverages far more long-term results than punishment. The list goes on.

Pivotal Power

"Give me a place to stand, and I can move the earth."
Archimedes

Your Challenge

- See power as the combination of energy, ability, authority, and influence.
- See power as unlimited, individual, and available to everyone. You can access power whenever and wherever you are simply by pivoting your perspective.
- Finally, see power as renewable. You always have power to choose, if not the situation, definitely you have the power to choose your attitude.
- You also have the power to give away your power and to feel powerless. But that wouldn't be a good choice.

Checklist: Pivoting from Obsolete Power

Assumptions & Thoughts
- ☐ Everyone is competitive.
- ☐ Some have power and others do not.
- ☐ If you are powerful, you always have power.
- ☐ The power that worked in the past will work in the future.
- ☐ The same type of power works best in every situation.
- ☐ Power is best wielded rather than leveraged.
- ☐ I have no power because I do not have an organizational position of power.
- ☐ Position power trumps all other types of power

Behaviors
- ☐ I rely primarily upon one type of power.
- ☐ I attempt to control all the power or as much as I can.
- ☐ Using too much power.
- ☐ Not utilizing the power you have.
- ☐ Relying on a superior's power.
- ☐ Assuming a superior's power will excuse your mistakes.
- ☐ Assuming you have more power than you do.
- ☐ Assuming everyone uses the same definition of power.
- ☐ Spreading your power too thin – trying to do too much too quickly.
- ☐ Attempting to squelch another's power.
- ☐ Not recognizing and utilizing a massive but hidden source of power that you are expected to sense.
- ☐ Spending too much time looking back and analyzing how someone overpowered you.
- ☐ Glossing over past power failures.
- ☐ Assuming someone has power when they do not.
- ☐ Assuming someone will use their power to solve problems.
- ☐ Using your power primarily to build your own empire or ego.
- ☐ Challenging a superior's power.
- ☐ Failing to engage all your sources of power before beginning a critical project.

- ☐ Being unprepared for power surges in the surrounding environment.
- ☐ Not learning more about power when you have the opportunity.

TYPES OF POWER

"Power is needed to do the Impossible. The question is which power to use at what point and to what degree?"
Loren Murfield

One of the biggest mistakes leaders make is thinking of power as a single entity. Raven first began studying power in the 1950s. Today we understand that there are six types of power. Knowing each of these provides a platform to pivot our personal power to do what we never thought possible.

1. Position Power.
As we will discuss later in the Authority section, there is power that comes from holding a position. With the title, we are given authority to do certain things.

For example, as a college professor, I was given the power to teach college students. Without permission from a college, I had no access to the classroom as an instructor or professor.

In the same way, I know many speakers who volunteer to offer a free training over lunch to businesses. By volunteering, they can claim the position where that company was their client. By securing a paid consultant or trainer position, even as a contractor, they will increase their power to market to other companies.

We can pivot our power by seeking positions that increase our power. We can seek jobs in for-profit as either a full-time or part-time employee or as a consultant. Even earning a position as a volunteer could increase your power.

There are also paid positions in the not-for-profits arenas. Depending on your ultimate goal, volunteering to serve on a board or help the charity may increase your power by connecting with the right people or building your credentials.

In the end, securing a position and the title to with it, often helps leverage your power to do what others never imagined.

2. Expert Power

The old joke claimed that anyone who traveled over 50 miles to give a presentation was an expert. To some degree that was true because perception is often reality. Technically, an expert is someone who had earned elite status in their field. Practically, an expert is anyone who knows what you don't. We become the expert if we are the ones others look to for the knowledge and skills. If we need someone to create a logo, we turn to someone that knows how. If they have a solid command of the skills, we will likely consider them our expert.

We leverage expert power when we know so much and can do a skill so well that others hold us in such high regard that they brag on us. They quickly hire us and refer them to their friends and colleagues. We become their expert.

Therefore, to pivot our power, we hone the needed skills and acquire the cutting-edge knowledge. That last part is critical. We are not the expert if we allow the world to pass us by, resting on what we learned years ago to earn the expert status.

3. Role Model

It is one thing to hold the position of leader, but another one to be trusted and quickly followed. To accomplish that, we need to build such a good connection with others that they know, like, and trust us. We become a role model for them. They will do whatever we ask because they respect us and see us as someone they can emulate.

This type of power poses a challenge that the position or expert role doesn't. This demands personal trust and respect. Position power only requires trust from the hiring authorities. Expert requires trust that you know what you are doing. Role Model requires a trust in who you are, who you are becoming, what you are doing, how you are doing it, and why. You must be authentic, and your actions must be pure. This power is so tentative that one violation of their trust and your power may be diminished.

Role Model power is all about them and how they see you. They expect transparency because hiding who you are or what you are doing will erode their trust and minimize your power.

To pivot this power, hone your character and be authentic.

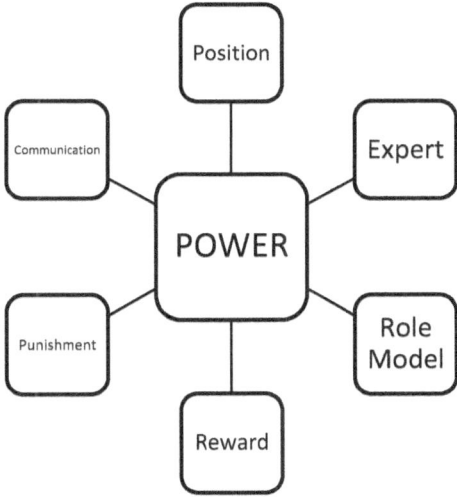

4. Reward Power

The first three types revolve around the type of leader you are. The next three focus on how you pivot your power.

Reward power is the fun part of any type of leadership, in a big corporation, as a social media celebrity, or as an entrepreneur. It is even fun as a parent or community leader because rewarding others means we give them something extra. It is more than just delivering a paycheck, which is fun but rather expected. Instead, rewarding is going above what was expected. It is usually for something they have done that goes beyond their usual responsibilities. It is an unexpected tip or a needed referral. As a parent, one of the best rewards a child can receive is hearing a parent brag about them to one of their friends.

We pivot our power to do amazing things when we reward others when they don't expect it. Start by offering compliments. Even a thank you goes a long way. Monetary rewards are nice but there are many ways to reward beyond cash. It might be offering to help with their project, helping their child, making a connection or a number of other methods. The important part is to provide more than what they expected.

Reward Power works well combined with Role Model Power. The leader who has a great relationship often gives compliments and desired responsibilities to those that follow. The rewards work not to bribe the followers but to show how much the leader cares.

5. Punishment Power

Punishment is used far too much by those who are insecure in their position and don't know how to build a good rapport. They operate out of fear and use punishment to motivate. It is often paired with Position Power and creates a negative culture.

It is tempting to say it is least powerful power but don't dismiss it. Much of our world demands compliance with punishment power. Violate the law, you are at risk of being fined or imprisoned. That makes a difference for many. Fail to pay your mortgage payment and you could lose everything you have invested in your house. Violate a trust with a powerful authority and they will sever the relationship. Even in our Homeowners Association, if we don't keep the mailbox painted, they cold fine us, and if we don't comply, sell our home.

At some point we must draw the line. We can be nice and try to build a rapport with individuals but if they cross too significant of a line, we must punish. We don't want to use this as a first choice, but boundaries must be maintained. If the consequences of violating the boundary, rule, or law is not upheld, others will not respect the boundary. That is when the punishment must be implanted for the wellbeing of the project or community.

The punishment doesn't need to be delivered harshly. Instead, as the leader, you increase your power by doing two things. First, breathe. Don't look for violations and nitpick tiny violations. Punish for belligerence, not misunderstandings. Second, administer punishment fairly and kindly. Don't enjoy it. Instead, explain that the process dictates the action. To do what you never thought possible, certain principles must be upheld.

Pivot your punishment power by using it sparingly and when you do, take the action for the betterment of the project.

6. Communication Power

Those that silver tongued individuals who can sweet talk anyone into anything hold a special power. So do the ones who know what they want and can articulate it clearly. Even more, those that can calm a conflict with a command of language and a caring heart will prevent costly problems.

Communication is more than exchanging thoughts. It is creating a shared meaning by negotiating with words and symbols. Communication is negotiation at its best between very different individuals. Those that develop their command of language and people skills mixed with a kind and giving heart, leverage their power to create pivotal success.

Pivot your communication power by learning to listen far more than you speak. Stop to understand first, suspend judgement, and then speak clearly and directly. We will discuss pivotal communication at the end of this book.

Pairing Power

We pivot our power when we can pair one of the first three types of power with one of the last three. Earlier I mentioned that those in position power often merge it with punishment power. Notice that creates a negative atmosphere that is often driven by fear. Those using that mix mistakenly think that fear drives the best success. Unfortunately, that isn't as often as they believe.

Mixing role model power with reward and communication power is a great mix because it builds rapport. Mix in expert power and you drive your success even further.

Now imagine someone in a position who wisely uses that authority to enhance their power. They are also an expert in their field. But mostly, they are so respected for their connection with their followers that they treat the leader as a role model. The leader rewards often and punishes only when needed and for the purpose of making the violator and the project better. In addition, they are effective communicators. Who wouldn't want to work with or for them?

Compassion Power

In *Pivotal Compassion* and *Pivotal Engagement* my wife and coauthor defined the power to pivot others lives by coming alongside of them to help alleviate their pain. When we help others, we build the rapport of the Role Model, fostering trust and enhancing a relationship. Our kind actions are rewards from a life that seems to be punishing them. Often the communication power is listening and understanding, practicing empathy that leads to compassion.

Unfortunately, many organizations don't see the hidden value and dismiss compassion as an unnecessary expense. They think it is too soft, giving everything to anyone.

That is not compassion power. Compassion is coming alongside someone to help alleviate their pain. It doesn't say you have to solve their problem. Instead, it is a balance between what they need and the resources you can lend at that time. No one can help everyone. In *Pivotal Apathy* I discuss several instances where we must say "No" in order to pivot to our next opportunity. It isn't harsh or mean but simply necessary.

At the same time, we don't shrug our community responsibility. We do what we can when we can. By helping another we leverage considerable power with that person but also those who are watching. They see us as a giver who isn't selfish. They want to reciprocate, helping us in return.

Balancing compassion is difficult and saying "No," especially when they desperately need it. But with a clear sense of purpose, we can balance our compassion to pivot our power.

Checklist: Types of Power

What type of power do you use most?
- ☐ Position Power
- ☐ Expert Power
- ☐ Role Model Power
- ☐ Punishment Power
- ☐ Reward Power
- ☐ Communication Power

Pivotal Power

4 ELEMENTS of POWER

*"The most common way people give up their power is
by thinking they don't have any."*
Alice Walker

    The power to do what we never thought possible relies upon four critical elements: energy, ability, authority, and influence. All four work together to drive you to a higher level, doing what you didn't think was possible, and maybe even to doing what no one thought was possible.

    Without energy, we never get off the couch. Without ability, we have the passion but not the skills. Without the authority, we are charged up with energy and ability but can't get to where we want to go. Finally, without influence, we are recklessly charging through life spending our time doing things that have no meaning or effect.

    Let's take a quick overview before examining each one in-depth.

Energy

    While the outside-in world goes to war for sources of energy, pivotal leaders find many sources of energy that are limitless to power their success. We use that energy to fuel our ability to sense and seize the best opportunities. When we care about others to the degree that we are committed to alleviating their pain, it is then that we free them to maximize their ability.

Ability

Our energy is the force we use to leverage our ability to innovate and do what others never thought possible. In the modern world, we find that we have access to energy that is renewable and sustainable beyond anything we have seen before. Our challenge is to switch to the new sources of energy as quickly as possible.

Authority

We will likely increase our authority so others give us their permission to do what they never imagined could be done. As we are deemed more competent, credible, and of value in the life of others, they grant us authority. They listen to us because they value our knowledge, insights, and wisdom. They willingly do what we suggest or voluntarily follow our example because they have given us a position of authority in their world. We often call this role model power.

What is most confusing about power is that many say they want power but, in all reality, want authority so they have the ability (power) to reward themselves and others or punish anyone who stands in the way of getting their reward. This is the pivot allow us to thrive.

Influence

The end result of doing what we never thought possible is influence. As a noun, this is the result we desire on their behavior or attitude. To influence another, we have the desired effect on them.

The best influence is making the world a better place. To influence others to be the best person they can be and to help others do the same is the ultimate source of energy. That compassion for others, in both good and bad times, taps a number of energy sources that bring unmatched results. Those that touch the lives of others leave a legacy that others want to emulate. That influence sets the standard high, doing what few if any thought possible. That is the influence of Mother Theresa, Gandhi, Martin Luther King and Abraham Lincoln. Their influence is widespread and long lasting.

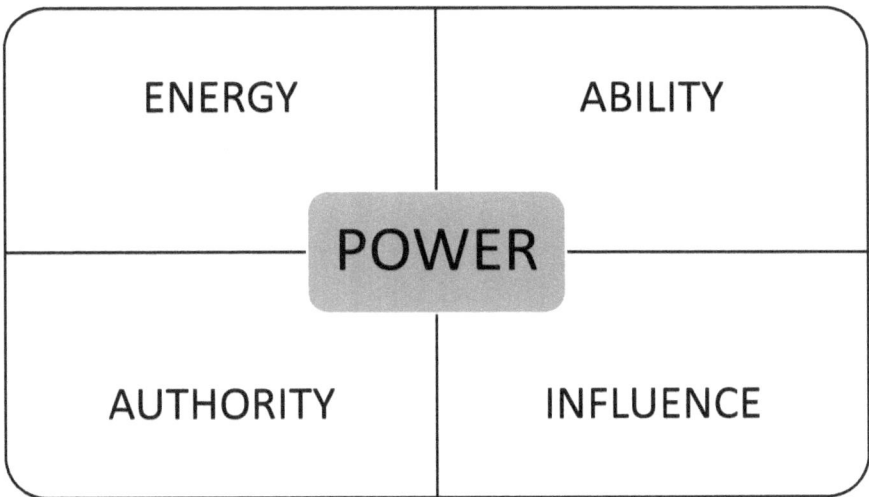

But for others, they seek an influence that is not as admirable. They clamor to be influential, to wield their power to make people do what they didn't want to do. They seek to destroy that which is significant just so they can say they were the one to do that. They are the assassins of energy and the arsons of ability. They are the ones that grind the wheels of progress to a halt before blaming anyone they can. That is an egotistical leadership disaster waiting to cripple others, organizations, and the world. That is not the best way to unleash the ultimate performance, production, and profits. It may not even be the best way to boost our own ego because it is destructive at its core.

As pivotal leaders at this critical point in the history of the world, we stand at the threshold of a revolutionary transformation. We have the energy, ability, and authority to influence our from what we are to what we ultimately want to become. It is our choice how we influence and to what level. It is our choice what legacy we will leave.

We power our pivot by tapping each of these four aspects.

Checklist: Elements of Power

Which element of power do you use most?
- ☐ Energy
- ☐ Authority
- ☐ Ability
- ☐ Influence

ENERGY

"The energy of the mind is the essence of life."
Aristotle

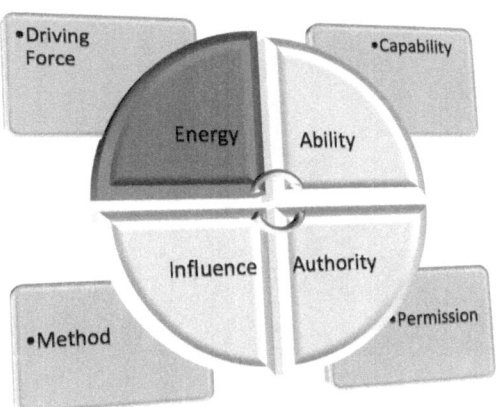

What is your driving force?

Where do you find your energy to do what has never been done before?

Without energy, we have no passion, drive, or determination because energy is the force behind the power. It is the desire behind learning, curiosity, and intrigue. Without the energy, talent and ability lie dormant. Without energy, authority is empty, and influence is a mere dream.

The encouraging part of energy is that it is renewable, not limited. There is an endless amount of energy available for those willing to learn how to generate their own energy. It isn't a scarce resource to be fought over but rather a plentiful supply that can be generated with excitement, dreaming, and collaborative synergy.

Since energy is renewable, even if you do not have the energy now, you can find and tap it. From there, you can do great things. Just do not expect that you can rely on someone else to give you the energy. Tapping the energy and using it becomes your choice, not someone else's choice for you.

Energy Defined

We see the power of compassion beginning with the potential to do something great, innovative, and what otherwise couldn't be done. Energy is a fascinating study. Let's take a deeper look before bringing it back to a workable definition.

<u>Potential</u>

"Mostly it is used in science to describe how much potential a physical system has to change." Wikipedia.com.

As pivotal leaders, we thrive on potential. We know that we have potential beyond what most expect of us. That is, in part, because we ideas that are loaded with potential. In fact, we have more ideas than we can possibly develop in the course of our lifetime.

Potential is the blue oceans of opportunity described by Kim and Mauborgne in their 2005 book by that name. We find opportunity, which is potential, not in the bloody waters of competition but in the blue oceans filled with fish.

Energy is potential because it is what is possible. The opposite is that which is impossible. Notice that we find potential from pivoting our thinking away from obstacles to opportunities, from impossible to possible, from despair to hope. Also notice how we feel when we pivot that thinking.

Anyone who has gone through a contentious divorce that they didn't seek knows the level of despair and depression that accompanies the experience. We lose hope when our dreams are shattered. At that point, all we want to do is isolate from others, hunker down, and survive to live another day. Unfortunately, that last one is questionable for some. When we lose our dreams, we can't imagine better days. There is no energy to anything. No wonder so many people are tired, drink too much, eat too much, and exercise to little. They have no energy.

But when we begin dreaming, something miraculous happens. We lift our heads, get up, find a bounce in our step, and a sparkle in our eyes. We find our energy when we envision something better than what we have right now.

That energy is hard to control. We think bigger with a dream. A dream is that wispy, not completely clear, promise of the future. It is the emotional first half of a detailed vision. With that dream, our brain and entire being pulses with energy as we contemplate how we can make it a reality. No wonder we quickly tire of the status quo and reach higher for what we ultimately want.

That is the potential of energy. With that energy, nothing is impossible, at least in our minds. We can imagine anything.

Now combine your personal energy with another like-minded individual. They have tapped the potential of their dream and are as excited as you are. Imagine the intensity of working together. Imagine putting your energy with theirs to work on a mutually satisfying dream. Now imagine the synergy that is generated, multiplying instead of simply adding.

Wow!

Do you sense the potential?

Now consider the opposite. Most individuals have more potential than they realize. They work in organizations that cannot see it, in part, because the individual doesn't appreciate their unique value and has quit dreaming. No wonder they become disengaged at work. They are disengaged in life.

Your Challenge

Where are you disengaged in life?
- ☐ Work
- ☐ Home
- ☐ Finances
- ☐ Health & Fitness
- ☐ Intellectual Learning and Growth
- ☐ Emotional Stability and Intelligence
- ☐ Social Connection
- ☐ Spiritual Connection

Capacity

Digging deeper we find that energy is also the capacity designated by its nature.

> "Energy, in physics, is the capacity for doing work. It may exist in potential, kinetic, thermal, electrical, chemical, nuclear, or other various forms. There are, moreover, heat and work—i.e., energy in the process of transfer from one body to another. After it has been transferred, energy is always designated according to its nature. Hence, heat transferred may become thermal energy, while work done may manifest itself in the form of mechanical energy."
> https://www.britannica.com/science/energy

Power and energy is the capacity to get things done. Without splitting hairs here, I want you to see that there is energy in the idea or opportunity. There is also the same amount of energy in denying the opportunity or dismissing an idea.

Now notice that how caring works to generate energy by converting the negative into the positive. Compassion is coming alongside another to help alleviate their pain. It may be intense, traumatic pain or an irritating, persistent frustration. Either way, your energy has the capacity to help them rise above that pain to dream again.

Notice the transformation characteristics of energy. As leaders seeking to exceed our own and other's expectations, we can convert the frustrations and failures into success. Lafair (2009) detailed how to convert the negative energy of broken family patterns into powerful personal characteristics.

Your Challenge

Look at the negative things in your life. How do they have the power necessary to fuel your ultimate accomplishment?

<u>Transferable</u>

Collaboration is critical to doing what we never thought possible. You've read it earlier, "Great things happen when good people work together." Together, we pool our energy to create opportunities much bigger than we could on our own because energy is transferred between objects and between people.

"In physics, energy is a property of matter and space, objects and fields. It can be transferred between objects and can also be converted in form."

Without going into a deep dive here, understand that energy is contagious, and in that sense, transferable. When we are around others who are encouraging, creative, and positive, we catch the fire and want to do more. At the same time, look at what happens when we are around negative, critical, complaining people. The only thing we want to do is run away. Whether positive or negative, we must be careful about who we are around because their energy will transfer to us.

"Energy is the essence of life. Every day you decide how you're going to use it by knowing what you want and what it takes to reach that goal, and by maintaining focus."
Oprah Winfrey

<u>Redirected - Not Destroyed or Created</u>
"It cannot, however, be created or destroyed."

The energy that we hold isn't going away, it will simply be redirected. If we don't pursue something significant, we will transfer that energy somewhere else. It might be positive or negative. It might be a positive influence or destructive. It might also be using that energy to read social media posts, play solitaire or complain about world news. Recognize that when you don't seem to have energy, you actually do but are redirecting it to something far less significant.

I have a hunch that many people are committing suicide in increments every day. They have given up on their dreams and redirect that energy to very slowing destroying their lives through short-term behaviors. They seek immediate pleasures at the expense of long-term health. They shop and put themselves in debt. They drink instead of exercise. They spend time with caustic friends instead of seeking positive ones.

Examining this definition, we come to see that energy is the potential and the force that drives our dreams and fuels innovative success. Without potential, there is no desire or drive.

Your Challenge
How are you redirecting energy toward negative results?
How are you redirecting energy toward positive results?

Knowing Our Why?
Simon Sinek is a widely known management consultant who gave one of the most popular TED Talks on "Start with Why." Sinek argues his golden circle of why, how, and what explains why some leaders and companies are able to inspire and why some are not. Sinek says that every single person and business on the planet knows *what* they do. We all know what product or service we provide. Going to the next level, some know *how* we do our business, whether it is a value proposition

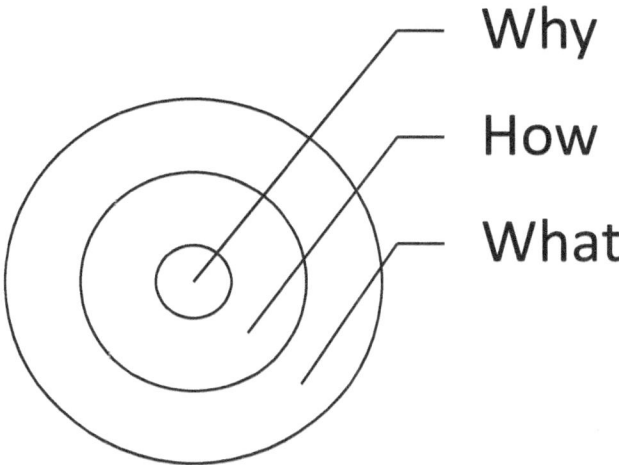

or a proprietary proposition or something else. Going to the center circle, Sinek notes that many people do not know why they are in business.

Applying this to individual energy, once we crystal clear on why we are seeking to do what others never imagined possible, we can do tremendous things. Once we know why others want and need something, we can create popular and successful products and services that many can't imagine because they didn't notice and listen. Understanding our why and theirs is critical to seizing our ultimate opportunity. It is incredibly powerful because it generates so much energy.

Your Challenge
Know your why. I'm reshuffling the questions to help you get to your why.
What is your ultimate opportunity?
Why is it so important to you?
How will that make a difference in the world?

Sinek's Golden Circle of Why
Many fail to recognize their purpose, cause, or belief. They do not understand why they are pursuing their ultimate opportunity, what gets them out of bed, or why anyone should care. This is an outside-in

model, working from the *what* to *how* and finally to the why. Those that inspire both inside and outside of the organization work in an inside-out model that generates massive energy that empowers radical success.

At the same time, some know exactly why they are seeking the ultimate. Unfortunately, their energy is driven by sinister intentions. They lie to business partners and associates get what they want.

In the end, others are pretty good at detecting self-centered individuals. No one enjoys being cheated or used. Notice what that does to our energy.

Instead, compassion is the best strategy because it generates considerable energy. When you help someone convert the negative to the positive, they will have an overwhelming desire to help you. They will be loyal as long as you are genuine. That synergistic energy will help you power your ultimate success.

Your Challenge

Are your intentions selfish?
Do you What is your ultimate opportunity?
Why is it so important to you?
How will that make a difference in the world?

The Outside-In Model

Many think they are doing the right thing by listening to others. Unfortunately, obedience doesn't generate nearly as much energy as compassionate collaboration. People lead their lives trying to be popular, pleasing people, and sacrificing their desires for the group. While it is good to be community minded, we cannot allow ourselves to reach the tipping point where we live for them and forget our dreams. Outside-in living doesn't generate nearly as much energy as Inside-Out living does.

Let's ask the difficult question. How much energy do you have when someone tells you what to do? Probably not a lot.

Now let me ask a follow-up question. How much energy do you have when you are working on something you want to do?

Is there an energy difference? Of course, there is. We all have far more energy when we are working on our pet project instead of something assigned to us. We won't have as much energy if someone is ordering us against our will. That is in part because we probably don't want to do the task they assigned to us.

However, if the task is something that we ultimately want to do and we finally get permission to do it, that is an entirely different story. That becomes Inside-Out rather than Outside-In.

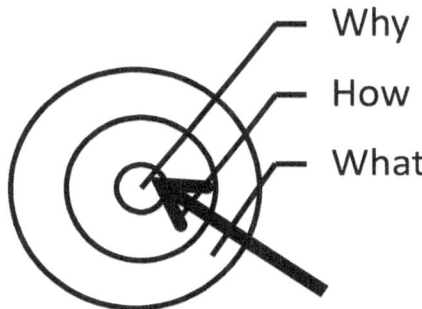

Let's be honest. Outside-In living doesn't generate as much energy. It is far more difficult to bring energy to the job when someone is dictating to us. However, when we are working on our own ideas, we generate massive amounts of energy. Let's see how that works.

The Inside-Out Model

To live Inside-Out is to work from the core of your being to do what you ultimately want. Some, maybe many, will look and wonder how you did it. What they don't understand is why and how.

I pivoted my life from chore boy to Ph.D. because I knew I wanted much more. But I made a critical mistake that people couldn't understand. It turned out I was trying to live Outside-In because I had no clue who I was, what I wanted to do, or how to do it. I was lost.

When lost, we don't have an inner compass to guide us so we look for outside help. That's where we run into trouble. Who do we listen to? How do we know we are doing the right thing? Will their advice work for us?

My problem was that I didn't have someone who could successfully guide me through the difficulties. My parents threw out a possibility, but I had concerns I couldn't discuss. So, I got did what others suggested, got a job, and tried to stick with it.

At that time, I was living with the notion that if I just worked hard, everything would turn out well. That was a lesson repeatedly taught throughout my life. In other words, be obedient and the system will treat you well.

Unfortunately, that didn't prove true. Too often I was left out or overlooked even though I had done my part. I even went beyond what most did in being obedient, yet the system wasn't fair.

At that point, I realized I was crazy to continue in that system. That's when I started to make my own choices. Notice that obedience doesn't allow us to make significant choices. I couldn't answer, "What do I ultimately want?" because I didn't know who I was. Not knowing my why blinded me to my unique value and ultimate potential. How could I make a choice when I didn't know the legitimate options?

Gradually, as I allowed myself to dream and explore, I saw a vision emerging from my very core. I began to see my why. I love helping people make the significant pivots in their life. I enjoy helping them find their energy to exceed the expectations of others. That came from a very negative place. I hated my days as a chore boy. Instead, I dreamed of pivoting to doing significant things that made a big difference. That's why I got involved in the church, went to Bible College, and considered the ministry. But my why wasn't the "what" of preaching. My why was pivotal transformation. As I understood that, I recognized that the parish ministry wasn't right for me. Two decades later, I also realized that academic teaching wasn't the appropriate what either. Neither allowed me the freedom to fully live my why. As an entrepreneur and executive coach, I am free to unleash my ultimate because no one is squelching my energy by telling me what I can and cannot do.

In the process, I transferred the energy of a dynamic preacher and the intellectual learning of an academic professor into a balanced approach to business and personal transformation. With that energy, is there any wonder why I could write 29 books in 14 years? Is there any wonder why I could write 8 books in one year, 6 in another?

Notice that I have lived an Inside-Out "Why => How => What" life. Once I discovered my why, I was no longer lost in the Outside-In world of obedience to what I found to be an unfair system.

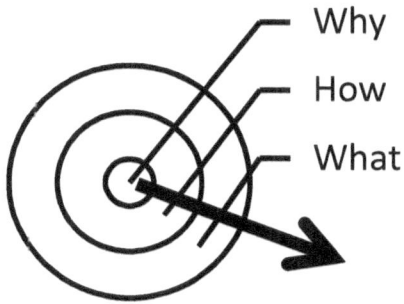

From the entrepreneurs I have coached, my story of transformation is common. They cannot work in corporate because the organization seeks to control, squelch, dismiss, or even destroy their why. Then they wonder why the entrepreneur is disengaged, unmotivated to carry out their commands. Corporate expects that what drives the employee how. They couldn't be more mistaken.

Your Challenge

What is your why?

I know I asked that before, but the challenge is to dig deeper.

Why is that why so important to you?

Notice in my story, my why started with the spiritual connection. But drilling down, I learned that I felt worthless as a chore boy and wanted to feel valuable enough to do something significant. In the process, I wanted to help others pivot through their sense of frustration to what they ultimately want. Think bigger and deeper to identify why your why is so important.

Great Leaders Know Their Why

Look at some of the great leaders. Oprah Winfrey built a media empire, Sir Edmond Hillary was the first to climb the world's tallest mountain and Richard Branson disrupted several industries from music to airlines to space travel. Why did they do it?

Let's examine what they have said about the innovation process.

"Create the highest, grandest vision possible for your life, because you become what you believe."
Oprah Winfrey

If the going is tough and the pressure is on, If the reserves of strength have been drained and the summit is still not in sight, then the quality to seek in the person is neither great strength nor quickness of hand, but rather a resolute mind firmly set on its purpose that refuses to let its body slack or rest.
Sir Edmund Hillary

"When I started Virgin from a basement in west London, there was no great plan or strategy. I didn't set out to build a business empire... For me, building a business is all about doing something to be proud of, bringing talented people together and creating something that's going to make a real difference to other people's lives."
Sir Richard Branson

Each of these great leaders knew their why. Oprah believed she could do more than menial chores, so she developed the highest, grandest vision possible for her life. She built an empire doing the same for her audience. Sir Edmond Hillary could identify with those that ask why he would push himself to such extremes. He enjoyed maximizing his potential, going to that point where he refuses to let his body rest in quest for the ultimate prize. Sir Richard Branson loves to have fun bringing people together to do great things. Notice how each reflects Simon Sinek's inside-out approach. They did great things because they knew their why.

To be the compassionate leader that leverages their power to innovate, you must first know your why. Is it just to get an end result? Is it just to make others happy? If so, that energy will likely fizzle out when others realize you are faking it. Authenticity is critical in developing innovative energy.

Energy is the first concept of power necessary to do what you never imagined. Tap your energy, convert it from the negative to fuel the positive.

Checklist: Energy

- ☐ Know your why.
- ☐ Dare to dream.
- ☐ Convert the negative to the positive.
- ☐ Recognize your potential.
- ☐ Choose to surround yourself with positive people.
- ☐ Choose your "what" based on your "why."
- ☐ Choose to Live Inside-Out.

Energy and persistence conquer all things.
Benjamin Franklin

Pivotal Power

ABILITY

"Intelligence is the ability to adapt to change."
Stephen Hawking

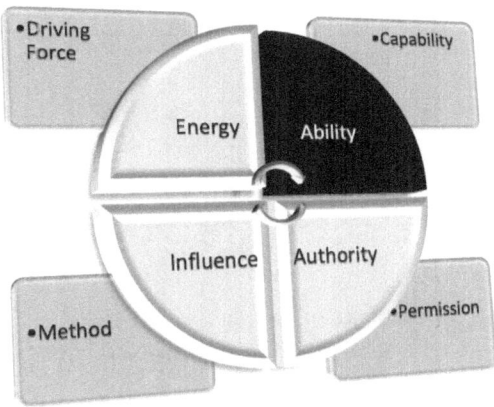

Stated simply, ability answers the question, "Can I do it?" That is the bottom line. If you or your team can't do it, you will not have the power to do whatever you want to do. The good news is that ability can be acquired.

According to Dictionary.com, ability is a synonym for capacity that we discussed in the previous chapter. Ability is also taken to mean aptitude, capability, and knack.

Many fail to innovate and leverage their power to do what they never imagined because they doubt their abilities. It isn't a question of whether or not they have the ability but rather that they recognize and appreciate their abilities.

In this chapter, we will discuss four elements that affect our ability to realize our ultimate dream. First, we discuss our self-concept, followed by self-awareness, self-esteem, and self-disclosure. However, before that we need to discuss knowledge and skills.

Knowledge

To develop our ability, we need several types of knowledge. First, we need to know what we know we know. Then we need to know what we don't know. Then we need to know what we thought we knew but didn't, before recognizing that there are things we don't know because they are unknown.

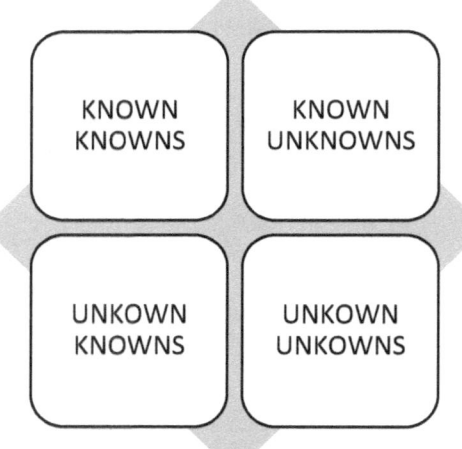

KNOWN KNOWNS	KNOWN UNKNOWNS
Know what we know	Know what we don't know.
UNKNOWN KNOWNS	UNKNOWN UNKNOWNS
Don't know what we thought we knew.	Don't know what is unknown at this time.

First of all, we need to appreciate what we already know. As we contemplate our ultimate opportunity, it is easy to be overwhelmed and say, "I can't do this because there is so much I don't know." But when we stop and consider what we do know, we build our confidence and ability.

One of the challenges I provide to my clients is to list what they know on a particular topic. At first, they doubt they know very much but as they start writing or talking, the list quickly grows. We know far more than we often think we know.

Second, we then tackle what we don't know. The good news is that with the internet and our smart phones, we can quickly find many of the answers.

One of the most critical traits of a successful person is one who is willing to ask for help. Warren Buffet is known for his ability to say he was wrong. In the same way, we need to be able to say that we don't know. When we do, we provide a positive energy because that gives us a point to start. Opposite of that is the energy draining tactic of claiming they know when they really don't. That is the precursor to a problem.

Third, this is very important. We often need to unlearn much of what we knew to do what we never thought possible. That means breaking the rules. I mentioned earlier that Albert Einstein had to break the rules of Newton who was the known and trusted theorist at the time. Einstein had to unlearn what he had relied upon.

This is a difficult issue for many, especially as we age. We build our careers gathering a massive amount of knowledge about a number of subjects. But then the world changes rapidly and radically, eliminating the need for much of our knowledge. That is frustrating but that doesn't matter. To continue to provide value, we must be willing to unlearn some of our best practices because they are now outdated.

Fourth, we also need to recognize that there are somethings that we don't know because they haven't been invented or discussed. They are unknown. For example, we don't know what next year will bring. We can guess but we simply don't know what we don't know.

Your Challenge

List the types of knowledge you bring to your ultimate opportunity. Put them in the following categories:

- ☐ Technical Innovation
- ☐ Content/Subject Matter
- ☐ People necessary for the project
- ☐ Project Management
- ☐ Psychological Motivation
- ☐ Cultural Considerations
- ☐ Political Nuances
- ☐ Legal Considerations
- ☐ other

Skills

Applying that same four-part matrix of knowns and unknowns, we assess our skills. We have many skills that we are aware of. However, there are also skills that we could excel with but have had no experience with, so we simply don't know. There will even be skills that we used to be good at that we haven't honed and are not as good as we thought. Then, especially with technology development, there are skills that we have no clue about because there is no need for them at this time. For example, a hundred years ago no one could imagine the skills necessary to program a computer. It was an unknown unknown.

Once again, I challenge my clients to assess their skills. In working with a recent college communication studies graduate, he struggled to understand what he could do with his major. In response to my query, he immediately said he was good with people. Over the years, I had heard that multiple times, so I knew I needed to dig deeper. He explained what he meant and how he was able to assemble teams that were productive. Digging even deeper he also revealed that he is good with handling money as he had been a grocery store checker during college. He had dismissed that skill thinking that anyone could do it. By the end of our work, he had secured a position as a bank teller and received praise for his work from his supervisor. The process of working through his competencies helped build his confidence and expand his skills. Since that time, he has been given additional duties that allowed him to expand his abilities.

That is what each of us wants and needs to push ourselves toward our ultimate opportunities. When we hone our skills and develop new ones, we increase our energy to do what we never thought possible. In the process, we often surprise others who proclaim, "I never thought you could do that."

Your Challenge

Now list the skills you have in those same areas.
- ☐ Technical Innovation
- ☐ Content/Subject Matter
- ☐ People necessary for the project
- ☐ Project Management
- ☐ Psychological Motivation
- ☐ Cultural Considerations
- ☐ Political Nuances
- ☐ Legal Considerations
- ☐ other

Look back over the knowledge and skills you have listed. Focus on what you currently know. Notice the energy your feel when you realize, "I can do that." Then notice the energy you sense when you realize, "I can learn and develop that skill."

Next, we discuss each of four critical elements in developing our ability: self-concept, self-awareness, self-esteem, and self-disclosure.

Checklist: Ability

Increase your ability by increasing your
- ☐ Knowledge
    - o What do you know?
    - o What do you know you don't know?
    - o What did you think you knew but realize you didn't?
- ☐ Skills
    - o What skills do you know you have?
    - o What skills do you need to hone?
    - o What skills do you need to acquire?
    - o What skills do you need to hire to leverage?

Self-Concept

"Too many people overvalue what they are not and undervalue what they are."
Malcolm Forbes

Self-Concept is the mental image we have of ourselves. Notice that image is visual as well as emotional and relational. When we think of ourselves, we often see a scene playing out where we play the role of the hero, victim, or villain. We may also see ourselves as playing a bit part, easily eliminated, and just lucky to be in the scene.

Notice how that self-concept either generates incredible energy or dissipates it depending on the conversation we have with ourselves. If make a mistake and say, "You idiot" it won't generate great energy. Instead, if you say, "Oh, that's not right. I'll try again . . . I knew I could do it!" Notice the difference?

As an author of both fiction and nonfiction, I recognize the power of a great story. One of the ways a character emerges as the hero is by seeing themselves in a different light. Audiences enjoy the transformation of Sansa Stark in *Games of Thrones* from a bratty child and sexual assault survivor to a strong leader. Who can forget Elle Woods in *Legally Blonde* who transformed her self-concept from blonde bimbo to savvy lawyer? Granted, she may not have seen herself that way, buts he emerged as the hero who did what others never imagined. Those stories are popular because they show the person overcoming a negative image of themselves.

Oprah Winfrey's transformation form an impoverished kid boiling clothes and suffering abuse has inspired millions. Even after she pulled herself up, earned her education and started work as a news reporter. Just when we would expect that her transformation was complete, she was fired. Imagine how she felt. Imagine the negativity that must have crept into her resolve. Imagine the image she must have seen in the mirror.

Everyone has doubts, especially when an organization that you value and build your hopes upon tells you that you are no value to them. Those experiences not only hurt, but they also tell us what we are not and toss us aside. In the process, we wonder if we are worthless.

Notice how the words and actions of others often shape our self-esteem. Malcolm Forbes, however, makes a powerful point. We overvalue what others tell us that we are not. We overemphasize the negative comparison with others rather than appreciating what we do well. That outward focus leads to a negative judgement and poor self-concept.

Instead, what happens when we appreciate our unique value. Oprah Winfrey had to dig down far beyond the negative she encountered. In the same way, each of us need to find what makes us uniquely valuable and focus on that. That is the purpose of my book and coaching program, *The Prize Inside*. I look back over my life and the one of my biggest regrets is that I allowed the doubts of others to shape how I saw and felt about myself.

Whenever we face a choice of reaching higher, our self-concept is going to provide the answer. If we see ourselves as competent and valuable, we will be thinking bigger and willing to reach higher. However, if we doubt our competence and value, we will likely stay at our same, frustrating level.

Oprah Winfrey is a great example because she had so many reasons to quit. But somewhere inside, she saw herself as far more than what others did. She pivoted her perspective to see herself as a powerful force in the world. That's where the energy came from to do what others never, ever imagined.

Notice that great stories don't just involve doing but are transformation of character. Being is as important, if not more important, than doing. When we change our self-concept to see ourselves as competent and valuable, we are on the verge of doing what others never imagined possible.

Checklist: Self-Concept

How do you see yourself? Choose only one.
- ☐ Hero
- ☐ Victim
- ☐ Villain
- ☐ Minor Role to Success
- ☐ Bit Part, hardly valuable.

Do you see yourself as ultimately succeeding?
- ☐ Yes
- ☐ No

Why?
_____

What actions do you see yourself taking?

How do you see yourself overcoming obstacles?
_____

What image do you have of yourself?
_____

Who do you see yourself being?
_____

Pivotal Power

Self-Awareness

"I think self-awareness is probably the most important thing towards being a champion."
Billie Jean King

Self-Awareness is how well you know yourself. When it comes to ability, self-awareness is checking to see if that self-image is accurate. Can we really do what we say we can do? But equally as important, what can you do that you are not presently aware you can do? In other words, self-awareness is matching your perception to your potential.

The Johari Window is helpful in leading with the power of compassion. When we care to look for our potential, and when others look at us, we all see through four panes.

	Known to Self	Not Known to Self
Known to Others	**Open Self**	**Blind Spot**
Not Known to Others	**Hidden Self**	**Unknown Self**

Applying this to a compassionate leader we see the following four selves.

The Open Self is when we read like an open book. We have no significant secrets and readily share with those that ask. We are authentic to those around us.

The Hidden Self is when we have secrets and hidden agendas. We guard ourselves against others that we don't trust. This may be because we are not authentic or when we don't feel valuable and protect ourselves from criticism. We hide because we are not confident, we will be treated with respect and valued for our potential.

The Blind Self is a potential landmine or gold mine. When we are blind to our potential, it is a hidden gift that will pay off nicely once we are aware of it. I am constantly amazed, amused, and encouraged to see people discover what they considered as "anyone can do that" worthless abilities as incredibly unique and valuable gifts. Their energy surges as they discovered hidden resources. At the same time, it is often very painful to help someone discover the way they have sabotaged their own success. They were blind to their own flaws. That can be ultimately freeing but comes with considerable pain. When that blind self is revealed and integrated into the self-concept, we enjoy doing far more than they believed was possible.

The Unknown Self is what nobody senses. The future is unknown. We don't know what opportunities will emerge or how we approach them. Just as we couldn't anticipate the 2020 pandemic shutdown, there is knowledge we do not currently know. At the same time, there is potential about each of us that we are currently unaware.

The challenge with self-awareness is that we often think we are being open and aware when we are blind to what could be known. Unfortunately, too often this is done to protect ourselves from perceived pain. Instead, the purposeful blindness also blocks our ultimate opportunities, fostering a tarnished self-concept that frustrates our success.

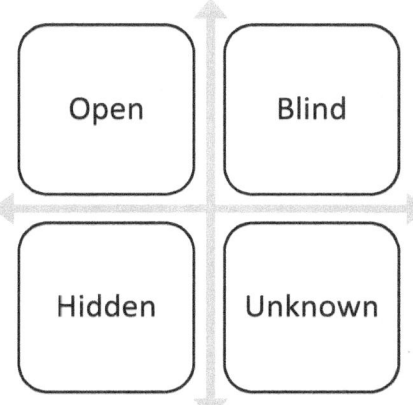

Checklist: Self-Awareness

- ☐ What areas are you completely open with others about yourself?
- ☐ What areas do you hide from others?
- ☐ This one is difficult. Stop and consider, what areas are you blind to that are causing problems?
- ☐ What potential abilities are you blind to?
- ☐ When you look into the future, what opportunities do you see? Sometimes we are blind and claim we don't know because we haven't looked.

Pivotal Power

Self-Esteem

*"Love yourself first and everything else falls into line.
You really have to love yourself to get anything done in this world."*
Lucille Ball

Self-Esteem is how we feel about ourselves. Those feelings come from how we value ourselves and perceive our value to the world around.

Too often we don't consider our feelings as part of success or business. Within the realm of corporate work or entrepreneurial enterprises, we quickly dismiss the idea by saying, "What do feelings have to do with anything? Just do the job." While the bottom line is performance, production, and profits, we cannot ignore that negative feelings are responsible for many problems. If we don't feel like we are worthy of success, we won't succeed. But when we feel confident, nothing seems impossible.

Instead, feelings serve as good barometers to measure our current and potential value. Feeling bad about yourself discounts your ability to pivot and seize phenomenal opportunities. Negative feelings equate to a perception of limited or minimal power. On the other side, feeling good about ourselves helps us to see many more opportunities. Instead of being pessimistic, you can be optimistic because, from your perspective, you see great opportunities.

Notice the difference. Feelings are based on our perspective. The situation doesn't change with good or bad feelings, but our perspective does.

But there is good news. Feelings are not our reality. They are simply our emotional reaction created by our perception. When we change our perception, we will likely change our feelings.

This is what is behind the concept of living inside-out that is detailed earlier and in *The Prize Inside*. Each of us holds the power to do what others consider "impossible" when we pivot our perspective to see our potential. We discover abilities and that changes our self-image and that changes how we feel about ourselves. As we discussed earlier, this is the energy that drives disruptive innovation. Much of that is fueled by being celebrated for our successes and being able to celebrate ourselves. After all, it's not much of a celebration if we don't feel good about ourselves in that moment.

The Inner Critic

Too often, we don't celebrate but rather criticize ourselves. Instead of focusing on what went right, we are obsessed with what went wrong. Pivoting to the positive unleashes our potential. That inner critic won't accept a celebration until the work was perfect.

Other times that inner critical won't enjoy a celebration because we cheated the process. Instead of working diligently, we "just slipped by" and gladly took the success. We cannot celebrate ourselves because we knew we let most of the opportunity slip away. Had we been more diligent, we could have done and had much more. That notion is stuck quietly away. The only way we celebrate in those situations is realizing we were fortunate not to fail.

Lurky deep within on other occasions is the critic who quietly whispers, "You aren't good enough. It won't work. Just forget about it." We listen and obey, leaving the opportunity untapped. We feel bad because we don't think we are good enough to be celebrated.

The inner critic often whispers quietly and constantly to create doubt and despair. It uses comparison to show that we aren't good enough compared to others or to what we should be. The inner critic has mastered the compliance gaining strategies discussed earlier, artistically weaving guilt and shame into every message. The end result is never quite feeling good enough or optimistic enough to do anything significant.

Even the most successful hear the critic. Garth Brooks said he is "insecure as hell." (Yahoo.com) In one interview I heard several years ago, he said he is very nervous each time he releases an album, worried that it isn't good enough or that his audience won't like it. All this despite having sold 157 million albums. He is the only artist to have released 9 albums that reached diamond status in the U.S. The Beatles had 6. (Wikepdia.com)

That inner critic may whisper, but when we take the big step and shoot for the moon, it shouts so loud it is deafening. Screaming that we are not worthy of great success, that critic's intent is to limit how good we feel about ourselves. That inner critic knows that once we have confidence, we will do the work and the success will follow.

The inner critic fears both failure and success. Instead of feeling powerful, we feel like a failure. You will read about powerful communication in a later chapter.

Fear and Anxiety

The inner critic works to demoralize us from real and imagined threats. Pittman and Karle (2015) write in *Rewire Your Anxious Brain* that "we feel fear when we actually are in trouble—like when a truck crosses the center line and heads toward us. We feel anxiety when we have a sense of dread or discomfort but aren't, at that moment, in danger." That critic also uses fear and anxiety in both the short-term as well as long-term.

But there is hope. Entire volumes have been written that detail the process of overcoming fears and anxiety. Legitimate threats, fears, can often be overcome by pivoting from the emotional to the logical, thinking through the situation. Tony Robbins lists 10 ways to overcome fear that include recognizing your fear, recognizing how you can use that fear to your advantage, recognizing your excuses, and surrounding yourself with success. (www.TonyRobbins.com)

Over the years I have found a couple ways that worked best for my clients and for myself. First, and foremost, identify what you are fearing. Your body is tensing but why? "Why am I afraid in this context?" Often, we are afraid of something that isn't going to happen.

I began teaching public speaking as a graduate student where I taught four lab sections. Students each were assigned to give 7 speeches as part of the required first year course. Given that public speaking is feared above death, some students delayed it as long as they could. We taught extemporaneous speaking where students were only allowed to use note cards with citations and key words. Many thought they would have felt more comfortable with a complete script and feared the limited notes. Our goal was to help them relate to the audience, not read a script.

Robbie sat in the back row and didn't appear overly nervous during our ice breaker speeches. But during her first big speech, her voice shook as did her hands. When she handed me her note cards, as all the students were required to make sure they were not scripting their speeches, I noticed the outside half inch of the stack of cards was soaked. She was so nervous that she sweat through those cards.

Over the course of the semester, we used a variety of methods to help her and others gain more confidence, pivoting their fear, to do what they never imagined they could do, give a great speech to any audience and feel good about themselves.

First, we identified the fear. Most people are afraid of being judged poorly. None of us want to look bad. Maybe that is why many report having nightmares where they are giving a speech in front of a full stadium naked. They feel exposed and afraid of what others will say. We countered that with logic. We openly talked about our goals and fears in the class. Bringing the fear of judgement to light, students quickly agreed that no one was in the class to laugh at another. Instead, we were here to support each other. In fact, even professional audiences want the speaker to succeed, except for a few caustic individuals. I encouraged positive praise for each student following their speeches. I would be the only one who gave a grade or offered ways they could improve.

We also focused on the process, explaining each step to make sure they could succeed. I checked their outlines in class and offered suggestions. I even allowed them to arrange for time during my office hours where they could do a dry run. I gave them every chance to succeed.

Along the way, I clarified the goal. They weren't expected to be perfect. This wasn't a performance but rather a public conversation where we created a shared meaning with the audience. I assured them I wasn't grading based on an occasional "um" or "ah" but how they connected with the audience and structured their presentation. I showed them that these filler sounds could be silenced by simply pausing silently. This helped them relax and be natural but polished.

On the last day, I reminded of them of where we started. As a class, we complimented each person on their progress. I specifically mentioned Robbie, who had made noticeable progress. Everyone agreed in spontaneous praise, to which she replied, with a smile, "But my note cards are still wet."

Notice the methods we used. We identified their fears. We countered those fears logically. We also clarified the process and articulated our goal. We forecast imperfections (the ums and ahs) and worked through them. In the process, they were surrounded with success. Instead of watching others to detect flaws, as an audience they connected with the speaker and supported them.

Imagine how they felt walking out of that classroom on the last day. Now imagine how they felt when they walked in on the first day. That is the difference we make when we pivot from our fears and anxiety to claim our confidence and do what we never imagined possible.

Overcoming anxiety is more difficult and is best left for the professional therapist. People have found a number of strategies to help, such as relaxation, meditation, and pharmaceutical drugs. Naturally, a psychiatrist is needed for the latter. We won't discuss relieving anxiety in depth because it is such a serious issue. Please seek out a professional to address anxiety. We want you to succeed.

Checklist: Self-Esteem

This checklist is a little different from the previous ones. Rate each of the answers with 1 as the least and 10 as the most.

- ☐ How do I feel about myself?
- ☐ How often do I feel valuable?

In what situations do I feel most valuable?
_____   _____
_____   _____

What actions do others see that tells them they are valuable?
_____   _____
_____   _____

What words or actions do I use that gives them the impression that I am not valuable?
_____   _____
_____   _____

What situations are most difficult for my self-esteem?
_____   _____
_____   _____

What methods can I take or build their self-esteem?
_____   _____
_____   _____

Self-Disclosure

"It takes a lot of courage to show your dreams to someone else."
Erma Bombeck

Self-Disclosure is openly sharing. Earlier we noted that communication is not merely transferring our thoughts but rather negotiating a shared meaning with a person who is much different that we are. Sharing, by its very definition is a compassionate act. We disclose our ability when we know sharing information can help solve a problem. Sharing is voluntary and valuable in the process of disruptive innovation because we leverage our power by inviting others to share their energy toward a valuable project. On the other hand, purposely not sharing valuable information with those we need on our team dismissed potential power and success.

But self-disclosure is dicey. We temp failure by sharing too much too soon and especially to the wrong person.

Disclosing to the Right People - Avoiding the Wrong Ones

Those of us with great ideas, and you are one because you are reading this book, must be careful about who we share those great ideas with. As Adam Grant says in *Give and Take*, (2013) it only takes one taker to ruin a collaborative team. It will be no surprise to you that there are many people who would love to steal your great idea. They are too lazy or insecure to find their own idea so they prowl conversations, befriend those with good ideas, to see how they can succeed by stealing yours. Although tempting, avoid those people at all costs. We dimmish our energy and power when we share with the wrong people.

However, when we disclose to the right people, we create the energy to do what we never imagined. Synergy multiplies energy. It's not just 1 + 1 = 2 but rather 1 x 1 = 11. The math doesn't make sense because when we connect in the right way with the right person at the right time, phenomenal things happen.

Disclosing the Right Information

We also diminish our energy and power by disclosing the wrong information to the right people. The point of connecting with collaborative partners is to do something significant. That requires that the energy flow without interruption. When we share something that is not helpful, it is as if we have unplugged the chord and disconnected the computer. To continue, we must power it back up. This can be a slight blip but can also be a significant power outage. Listen carefully, pivot your perspective to ask for clarification to avoid sharing the wrong information.

But when we know exactly what to say we make the critical connection that allows the energy to flow and fuel the fantastic success.

Think back and remember a time when someone gave you a compliment at the exact time you needed it. Remember how you were doubting yourself, but those kind words lifted your spirit and raised your chin. Feel the confidence that swelled within you.

Be that encouragement to someone else. Provide the message that they welcome at that moment.

Disclosing in the Right Way

Sometimes our intent is good, but our words don't reflect it. For example, a brother was visiting and was quietly noticing my framed diplomas. He returned to the conversation and said, "Of all of us 8 kids, and I think everyone else would agree, you were the last one we thought would ever be successful."

I was taken back but not in a good way. What I heard was that my entire large family saw me as a loser and doubted I would ever be successful. Maybe that was because I was too sensitive due to a poor self-concept and self-esteem from those early years. Imagine if he had approached it differently. "I'm impressed with what you have accomplished. Although we wondered about your potential in those early days, you have impressed us all." My reaction and that of everyone in the room would have been appreciated and even celebratory.

Disclose the information in the right way and you will create a tremendous flow of energy.

Disclosing at the Perfect Time

Great timing makes for great success. Bad timing, however, ruins the best of projects. Any athlete in team sports understand the value of timing for the perfect pass, defense, or leap. A little too early or late and the play goes from great to one that just missed. Often the difference is a millisecond. In the same way, saying the right thing at the wrong time misses the mark.

There is a right time for a compliment or to share a concern. Listen carefully and find the right moment and you will increase the energy of the relationship and leverage your power.

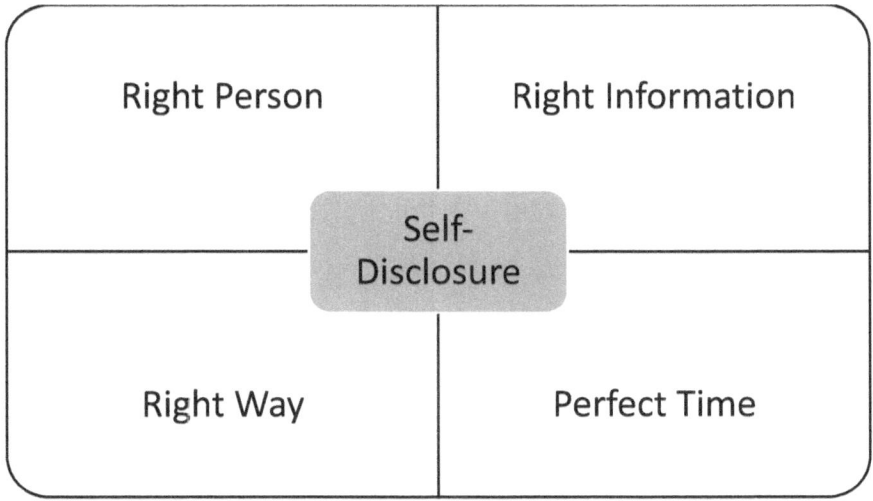

Other Concerns

Within the four aspects of powerful self-disclosure, I must mention place. Most self-disclosures are best delivered in private. Concerns over a project shouldn't happen in a committee meeting but rather in a private conversation. Once we bring it beyond the one-to-one interpersonal relationship, we risk embarrassing the other person. We also risk embarrassing ourselves.

If the other person isn't welcoming of the self-disclosure, it isn't appropriate. This isn't the time, way, information, or the person to share this information. It might only be one of those, but if it is, self-disclosure is inappropriate.

Why Don't We Self-Disclose?

Many are unwilling to disclose information for a variety of reasons. Some fear that they will look stupid. They worry that they do not know the right information or enough information to be valuable. Others are concerned about their image and reason, "It is better stay quiet than be exposed." Still others fear that if they do share, they will get into a conversation or relationship that they want to avoid. Then there are those that do not want to disclose for fear they will be ridiculed for exposing something that will cast them in a poor light. Then there are those times where we don't know what to say so we don't say anything.

This is where self-disclosure becomes so very difficult. "Do I say something or not? Will I make it better or make it worse?"

The key is to have the right intention and communicate that. Don't be afraid to ask if this is the right time to share your feelings or thoughts.

Another key is to always be ready to apologize if you were wrong about the time or place.

Why do We Self-Disclose Too Much?

We have all heard someone share something and heard the response, "TMI. Stop, you are giving me too much information." By providing that information, it places a blocker in the way of our future relationship. It is as if we have suddenly seen them naked. We cannot unsee that and every time we see them in the future, that is what we see. My youngest son had a great phrase for that. "I'm going to have to slaughter a pig to get that vision out of my mind." In other words, I'm going to have to see something much worse just to pivot from that vision.

So why so others disclose too much at times? Why do we do it? As you can see, self-concept, self-image, and self-awareness all factor into self-disclosure. If we are feeling insecure or desperate, we will likely offer information that shouldn't be disclosed. The entrepreneur who desperately needs investors is just as verbally clumsy as the nerdy teen that really wants a date for prom or the insecure boy that meets the gorgeous girl. It is like negotiation. The person who has the power to say "No" often finds it easiest to keep from divulging the wrong information at the wrong time to the wrong person or in the wrong way.

So, the key is to be confident in who you are and what you are doing. Know your value and you will have the power to make the appropriate comment at the perfect time.

Self-Disclosure and Innovation

Self-disclosure is critical to innovation, but some have difficulty with inappropriate disclosure. When we make the right comment to the right person at the right time and in the right way, we encourage innovation. It's not just a nice complement or a suggestion. Recognize that the perfect self-disclosure might be the rocket fuel needed to launch their success. At the same time, it could be like extinguishing their flame.

As an author, I'm an entrepreneur looking to do what I once imagined impossible. You can imagine that I'm excited when I release a new book. I know how many hours and how much thought it takes to develop an idea into a complete book. I also know the emotions I have experienced quietly secluded in my den for days and weeks sorting through the possibilities, choosing wisely, capturing my thoughts on the computer, before painfully editing every word, phrase, sentence, paragraph, and chapter. In the end, writing a book that will be significant to others, demands every part of my mind, body, and spirit.

Put yourself in my shoes and feel the emotions of completing that process. Doesn't it feel great?

Now imagine receiving your first copy in the mail. You beam with pride.

Then imagine showing your book to what you consider a trusted friend. What are you expecting to hear?

Of course, you want to hear that they are as excited as you are. Anything less and you will be disappointed if not demoralized. Everyone wants to be celebrated. If they are not, they likely won't do it again.

Unfortunately, even our trusted friends respond with self-disclosure that is inappropriate. Instead of being the perky cheerleader that we desire and need, they decide to play the tough critic, providing their unsolicited opinion to "help us."

That is a lie. They wipe their insecurity on the white carpet of our dreams simply to protect their fragile egos. Does that sound too harsh? Granted, it could be because they don't know better and haven't learned good social graces. However, in the end, they puff themselves up by finding our flaws.

Below are a few unsolicited comments people have given me in the last fourteen years of writing books. Each show a play for power or reveal their inabilities and insecurities. As Ruiz says in *The Four Agreements*, their comments say more about them than they do about me or my work. Take that to heart as you seek to do what others never imagine possible.

"Oh, you finally finished." They are implying that it took an inordinate amount of time for you to complete the book. They show their ignorance in tackling a significant project.

"Ok. Let me see." Pausing for about a minute, scanning the book until they finally find what they are looking for, "You have a typo on page 73." These self-appointed critics are not happy until they find a mistake. Notice they didn't offer a compliment first. Determined to show their superiority, they reveal they cannot be trusted. Why would anyone want to reveal that about themselves? They will defend it as simply trying to help but don't believe it.

"Why did you choose that color?" Again, casting doubt on my choice, they are trying to claim their superiority. Instead of saying, "Help me understand the process, what is your thinking behind this choice?" Even then, that is not appropriate for a first response. The first response should always be positive. Remember, self-disclosure is designed to foster energy, leverage power, and do great things.

"I don't like the font." This is blatant play for power. They offer their opinion without understanding the process used to come to the best decision. They efforts in market research and assume their opinion trumps everything you have done. Given you have followed the process, forget what they say. Better yet, forget about even discussing it with them in the future. They cannot be trusted.

"You should write a book about . . ." It seems everyone has an idea for a best-selling book, blockbuster movie, or radical innovation. They can only wish that you will take their idea and run with it so they can later claim, "That was my idea." Very few who offer this comment have the energy or desire, much less the idea that will break through. So why should we listen to them? They are disclosing this information out of their insecurity. In some ways they are jealous and other ways they are secretly hoping you will make them look good. There will always be "that person" who offer the unsolicited idea for selfish gain. Also notice they use the world should. I discuss that in *Pivotal Apathy*. It is a power term used to imply guilt. Don't let them "should" on you.

"That's too thick. I only read books less than 100 pages." This one surprised me. Why would anyone admit that they only take the easy road? By their comments, they are admitting that they avoid difficult ideas and projects. But they don't realize it. They simply think they are proclaiming who they are and what they like. They don't realize what they are self-disclosing to someone who has done far more in that realm.

Fueling Innovation

Now consider some of the comments that fuel energy, strengthen relationships, and power innovation even higher.

"Wow. I love it." You gotta love that energy.

"This is impressive. It must have taken a lot of work." They recognize the effort required and what you have accomplished.

"Can I buy a copy?" They and want to reward you for the efforts.

"Have you shared this on social media? I'd love to share it with my friends." They are so enthused with your success that they want to help you towards your ultimate goal.

These are your loyal friends and fans. They understand the process and are willing to share their joy with others. Celebrate those who celebrate you. They are the ones the energize us and make us want to go higher.

Your Challenge

Don't just impulsively react with self-disclosure. Make it meaningful by making it to the right person, with the right message, in the right way and at the right time. Remember, these were friends who will fuel your success.

At the same time, let see the self-disclosure of the self-proclaimed critic as being more about them than it is about you.

Checklist: Self-Disclosure

Before saying anything to anyone, recognize what it says about you. Also consider what they need to hear to fuel their ultimate success.

- ☐ Is this the right person to share this information?
- ☐ Is this the right information to share with this person in this situation.
- ☐ What is the right way to phrase this message?
- ☐ Is this the perfect time to share this message?
- ☐ Is this the right place to share this message?
- ☐ Are they welcoming this message at this time and in this way?

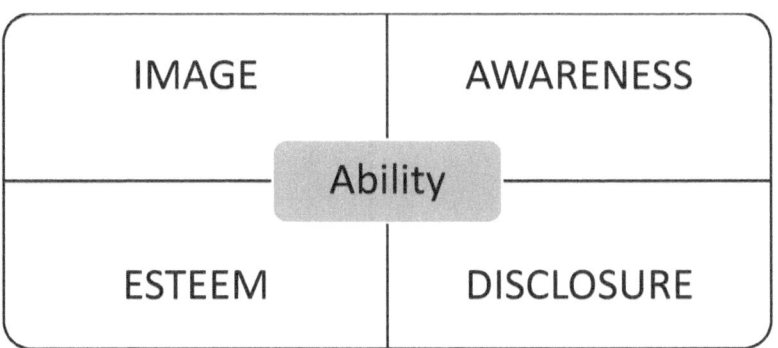

Checklist: Ability

In the previous pages you have the checklists for self-concept, self-awareness, self-esteem, and self-disclosure. They all work to create your ability. Below is your checklist for the entire ability section.

What is the imagine I have of myself?
_____

How aware am I of who I am, the unique value I offer, and the potential I hold to do what others consider impossible?

Circle the number that best reflects your awareness.

Unaware 1 2 3 4 5 6 7 8 9 10 Extremely Aware

How good you I feel about myself.

Pathetic 1 2 3 4 5 6 7 8 9 10 Fantastic

How well do I use self-disclosure?

Always Selfishly 1 2 3 4 5 6 7 8 9 10 Generously and Compassionately

AUTHORITY

"I have as much authority as the Pope, I just don't have as many people who believe it."
George Carlin

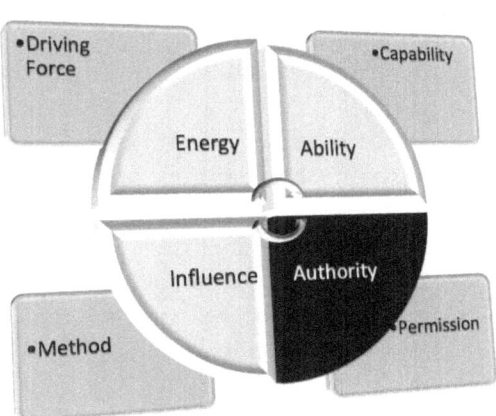

Authority is permission. To do what you never thought possible and then to do what other never imagined possible, often starts by giving yourself permission. Many never pivot and attempt crazy success because they don't give themselves permission to try, fail, or succeed.

Authority is defined as "the right or power to control, command or determine." (dictionary.com). We often associate authority with a position within an organization. With the title for that position, we know what we can do and what we are restricted from doing. We know our lane and stay in it. Either we have the authority, or we don't.

Notice how that perspective restricts rather than leverages power. First, without a position, you have no authority and therefore, no permission to do what others cannot imagine. Second, it requires obeying what someone else decides. Third, notice that to act without authority is to break the chain of command and threaten your position.

Power comes when we step into the authority. It is a purposeful and strategic action designed to accomplish great things. At times, it will take defying what others consider their authority.

Authority is a sensitive issue because it represents the radical pivot emerging in the present age. Each of us as individuals have a tremendous opportunity to defy the authority of organizations and start our own venture. We have the authority of essentially living off the grid and away from the reaches of most authority. Instead of applying for and being given approval to work for an organization, we give ourselves permission to find a way to do what we love and earn as much as we desire.

Even within organizations, today's employees have far more opportunities for jobs than they have ever had. More frequently than before, workers can choose to work in the office, home or remotely. They can choose to be a permanent employee, work temporarily in the gig economy, or become an entrepreneur. Technology and other innovative organizations have flattened the organizational chart, giving employees more choices for how, when, and even what they work on. Google is famous for allowing workers 20% of the time to work on their pet projects. With more choices in employment and even the nature of their work, authority has shifted. Once it was tied to position but today it is more likely to be associated with knowledge and skills. You have authority if you can do what the team needs to innovate. That changes the nature of work relationships and also the power balance in organizations.

Today leaders find incredible power in their connections. They develop team members instead of finding followers. The best entrepreneurs build tribes who willingly give their permission to lead, knowing the power is shared.

Permission

Notice the permission is based on sharing. Consider your behavior on social media. Notice how we all share our personal information and email in exchange for information and tools that help us maximize our abilities. We give them permission to send us tweets. In exchange, leaders give us permission to post on their social media sites. We form a community as we connect with others in the tribe. In the process, we create a community that is beneficial to all. It is no longer leader and follower but simply different roles.

One could argue the permission is the currency of social media. Without permission, we cannot build a following and cannot generate the desired income. Other individuals give us permission once they know we care about their pain. If we do not care, they do not trust us and refuse to give us permission to enter their world. If we do not generate energy in their lives, we do not help them find a way to leverage their ability. If we do not help them get the desired results, we will never increase our own authority. If we do NOT care, they will not engage.

Notice the pivotal paradigm shift. During the agricultural age, individuals worked their farms to meet their needs. They didn't worry about earning money, only providing subsistence for themselves. The Industrial Age, pivoted farmers into the cities to work for organizations that used permission as a motivation to move up the ladder to higher and higher positions. With each step came more responsibility based on the perception of ability. Without a position of power, one had little influence.

I gave myself permission to feel and experience all of my emotions. In order to do that, I had to stop being afraid to feel. In order to do that, I taught myself to believe that no matter what I felt or what happened when I felt it, I would be okay.
Iyanla Vanzant

With the computer and smart phone age, employees now have the authority to work for themselves. We can give ourselves permission to earn our own wage. Unlike previous generations, we have options and therefore, create our own position by giving ourselves permission.

During the 2020 pandemic, business were frightened about the outcome of granting employees permission to work from home. The critics believed in the antiquated Theory X model of Management. Employees must be controlled, and authority firmly established. Butts must be firmly in seats or performance, production, and profits would tank.

To their surprise, it worked. Employees not only largely responsible, but many juggled helping children also suddenly taking classes virtually and daycare back at home. Of course, there were some slackers but for the most part, employees rose to the challenge. But there are still those who cannot imagine how even a hybrid model can be sustained. Truth be told, those critics can't give themselves permission to believe that workers can be productive without someone in authority standing over them.

They don't believe individuals are responsible enough to have authority to make decisions. No wonder many don't give themselves permission to be an entrepreneur or to claim personal power.

Personal power is tapping our energy to develop our ability and give ourselves permission to do great things. We don't need someone standing over us, wielding power, and dictating decisions.

We discussed this earlier in the discussion on choice. Choice is giving ourselves permission to decide. Making our informed choice about our future is giving ourselves the authority to run our own life.

That might sound elementary, something that everyone should know. But granting ourselves permission is a critical step for anyone doing what they never imagined. It is taking control from those we have given it to, even when they didn't want it.

Listen to the language of those who claim they don't have a choice and you will hear, "That's not possible." "That's not an option." "There are other concerns." Notice the language used takes away the authority to take any other action.

Where do you give away your authority?

Excuses

Wayne Dwyer detailed 18 of the most common excuses used as justification for leading our own lives in *Excuses Be Gone* (2009.) These include:

It will be difficult.
It will be risky.
It will take a long time.
There will be family drama.
I don't deserve it.
It's not my nature.
I can't afford it.
No one will help me.
It has never happened before.
I'm not strong enough.
I'm not smart enough.
I'm too old (or not old enough)
The rules won't let me.
It's too big, I don't have the energy.
It's my personal family history.
I'm too busy.
I'm too scared.

Notice how these phrases prevent pivoting to the next, great opportunities by placing the present into an impossibility. The future is painted to be so far outside the reach of these resources that it cannot be done. It is impossible so why try.

But what happens when we give ourselves permission to find those resources? I believe we need to redefine the term "impossible." It simply means that "we don't yet have the resources." Anything becomes possible when we attain the ability and energy. Look at how we can change our lives with the cutting-edge knowledge and skills. Imagine what we can do with access to money. Notice how we pivot our perspective when we think, "all I have to do is _____." Notice it comes down to one item. Also notice that you are giving yourself permission to find that resource.

Many people my age complain that they don't have enough money to enjoy retirement the way they desire. Many are concerned that they cannot afford to retire.

A few years ago a financial planner held a lunch where he used the panic button to scare people into investing. He claimed that he studied the numbers and that the expenses of Medicare would soon surpass their social security. As I sat there, I recognized that he was missing the critical point. He assumed people would not give themselves permission to work even part-time following their retirement. Instead of wishing they had more money, they needed to figure out how to make more money without going back to a 9-5 job Monday through Friday.

Notice too many are wielding the power of authority when they claim, "I'm retired. I shouldn't have to work." At the same time, they will claim, "I don't want to be a greeter at Wal-Mart." Then notice what happens when someone gives them permission to find a better alternative. "You don't have to. What if you learned how to be a programmer? What if you started your own internet business? What if you tried something new? The point is to give ourselves permission to explore the unknown. We get stuck when we claim we don't have choices.

Now notice what happens when we tap our energy to pivot our attitude, knowledge, and skills to set higher goals. Instead of "cannot' we say, "maybe I can after all." Instead of "Why?" we say, "Why not?"

Instead of saying, "That's not possible" we say, "I see how it can work."

We have more power than we perceive.

Checklist: Authority

- ☐ Who already gives you permission to do what you ultimately want?
- ☐ What positions of authority do you already hold?
- ☐ What positions of authority would you like to hold?
- ☐ What do you need to give yourself permission to do to pursue your ultimate opportunity?
- ☐ What excuses do you use to justify not giving yourself permission?

INFLUENCE

"The art of communication is the language of leadership."
James Humes

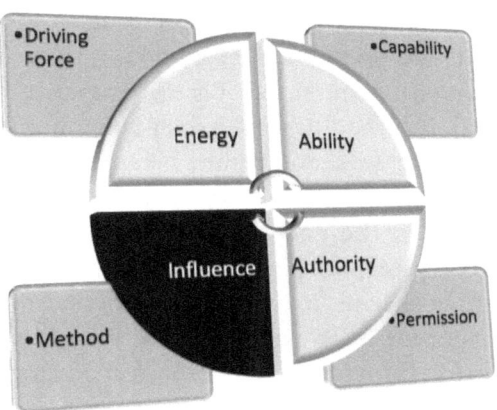

Profit is the end game of every for-profit business. Without the profit, we are no longer in business. Leveraging your power is the best approach to seizing your ultimate opportunity because compassion is the best business strategy, operation, and tactic to do what you ultimately want to do. Coming alongside another to help alleviate their pain unleash the ultimate performance, production and profit by building rapport, trust, and loyalty.

As entrepreneurial leaders we all want to have influence. We want to make the difference for any organization where we hold a position and in our personal lives. Many mistakenly think authority is what they ultimately desire but influence is much more. Influence is the end result. Authority is simply a means to an end. Remember, authority is merely the permission to make the decision while influence is the difference we make.

Influence

What influence do you ultimately want? In other words, when you lay your head down for the last time, what will you want to have accomplished? What do you want to be your legacy? When others think of you, what do you want them to say about you?

The end result of pivotal power is making the world better by solving significant problems. Notice that is far different than a greedy, selfish life. We succeed when we help enough others pivot to their ultimate succeed. We don't succeed by taking from them to get what we want. Compassion is the secret ingredient that self-centered people don't understand. It is the fulcrum in the pivot and the leverage. Move it to the right place and the end results is far easier.

Other less noble methods may make a quicker and more profitable sale but, in the end, those tend to flame out quickly. For example, a stereotypical salesperson goes for the immediate sale. Let's say they use their charms to convince someone to buy. But in the process, the customer feels like they were sold a bill of goods. How does that work for future sales? Often a forced first sale cripples the opportunity to make a repeat sale because they don't focus on the ultimate influence. Had the salesperson leveraged that first sale, maybe offered them a good deal, they might have created a loyal client that would have multiplied their residual sales.

The Pivotal Leader understands how that requires tapping their energy of connection and identification, affirming the significance of that other person or organization while working to collaborate instead of complete. The end is someone that wants to work together toward mutual satisfaction. Instead of applying their force to make one sale, they care enough to alleviate their other's pain and end up making multiple sales.

The end result is the influence we really want. Too often people do not think big enough or reach high enough. They settle for ordinary when they could enjoy the ultimate success.

Many do not give compassion a chance. They dismiss it outright because it operates out of a radically different paradigm. Others give it a half-hearted effort and quickly dismiss it claiming it didn't work. Many are heard to say, "I tried that once and wouldn't make that mistake again." Still others think they are using compassion when they are just putting a veneer on the old selfish, competitive paradigm of selfishness. They are using sympathy instead of empathy and wondering why their thinly veiled efforts are not getting the results.

The influence of compassion is authentic connection. As we defined earlier, influence is the result of maximizing our abilities when we tap our ultimate source of energy. With compassion, we are seeing what happens when we identify, affirm, and engage the abilities of others based on the energy they have available. This is an inside-out rather than an outside-in process. By affirming that others have the potential, the ability to do far more than most recognize and maybe even more than they see in themselves, we as awaken a significance in them that has the power to deliver powerful results.

That influence is both pivotal and disruptive. It is a transformation, not just a transaction.

Meanwhile, individuals fostering an authoritarian, top-down, competition, obsessed with control and obedience cannot see outside of their position and punishment power.

That forced influence is limited because it is an outside-in method that guarantees a disconnection with their energy and usually results in powerlessness. That is why obedience and control as a prevalent leadership or management model simply is not the most effective method, model, or tactic.

To fully comprehend and leverage our pivotal power to lead, we need compassion. That involves three aspects of influence, stimulus (their why), impact (their how) and result (their what).

Stimulus (Why?)

Why do you want to seize your ultimate opportunity?

In my first book, *Pivotal Small Business*, I take readers through the eight gears to their ultimate success. Critical to their success is determining very early why they want to go to their ultimate destination.

We need to carefully scrutinize our why. If we lying to ourselves, we will only sabotage our efforts. Sooner or later, we will be exposed to the world, or at least, to those most significant to the project.

- What do you ultimately want?
- Why do you want it?
- Why is it your top priority?

Impact (How?)

Pivotal Power is compelling and relentless yet soft and compassionate. As you have learned, it is not competitive or ruthless. In the end, you will be known as much for how you lead as what you accomplished. That will speak volumes.

As compassionate leaders, we think bigger and reach higher by connecting, collaborating, and creating. In that connection, we help others do what they never thought they could do and often what others never thought could be done. It is the result as well as the method that makes the difference. Compassion is about caring for our people but it is also about caring about innovative results. The incredible aspect of compassion is that it does both and proves to be a better model than any other. We get the best results when we care enough to come alongside another, take the time to identify their pain and then work to alleviate it. It is then that we can collaborate most. Our teams respond best when we have helped them solve important problems. It is then that they are engaged. They want to collaborate. They are willing to accept a seemingly impossible challenge because they know you support them. They know you would not give them a goal that wasn't important. Also, they know they can trust their team because of the culture you have established.

Forget the cultural myths that the good don't always die young and good guys don't always finish last. Actually, as Adam Grant writes in *Give and Take*, the best companies are led by the givers. Takers sabotage the results for selfish gain. Some do win, but ultimately the companies can't survive.

- How do you want to lead?
- How do you want to make a difference?
- How do you want to be remembered?

Result (What?)

The ultimate result is making your ultimate dream a reality. It is finding that phenomenal opportunity that you doubted was possible. It is becoming the leader some may thought you would never become or making a difference they doubted could be done. In the end, the result of influence is your legacy.

- What do you ultimately want to do?
- What difference to you want to make in the world?

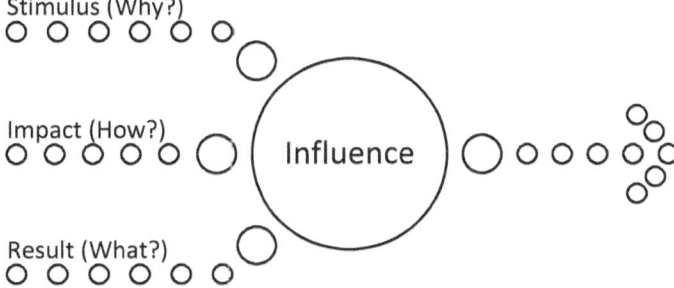

Checklist: Influence

- ☐ Who do you want to influence?
- ☐ How do you want to influence them?
- ☐ Why do you want this influence?
- ☐ What difference will this influence make in your world and theirs?

Checklist: Pivotal Leadership Power

Ask yourself the following questions each morning.

- ☐ What is my approach to leadership?
- ☐ Why am I leading?
- ☐ Why would anyone join my team?
- ☐ How do I view myself as a leader?
- ☐ How do I feel about myself as a leader?

With every decision, ask yourself:

POWERFUL COMMUNICATION

Words create meaning.

Notice the language we hide behind within the inability to recognize our choices. We claim, "I can't help it. That's just the way I am." Notice the powerless language of "not." They do not because they claim they cannot when it really means they will not. They have made a choice that prevents them from doing what they never thought possible.

Notice that it really isn't "they" but "we" and "I." I take the action. I fail to see I have a choice.

I taught the college course Interpersonal Communication for several semesters. The course is designed to study and apply how to improve our relational conversations. Unfortunately, too many students neglected to see the choice for improvement. They responded with either "That's just the way I am" or "I think I'm doing pretty well."

Notice how those messages squelch the opportunity to become much more. They see no need to make the choice to improve because they think they are "good enough."

Also notice how that phrase, "that's just the way I am" serves as their threshold for survival. They are not choosing to pivot to become the best they can be but are content where they are. They are not looking to leverage their ultimate power, but to settle for what they currently have. They are also not willing to change their belief that they need or want to do any more than necessary. As we discussed earlier, they may not want to exert the effort or challenge their ego. Whatever the reason, they do not see the opportunities vividly. They are blind to the opportunities.

In the same way, those who see themselves as imprisoned to circumstances or history, often say, "You don't understand. I'm just not that person." They rely on the nots to define who they are and the opportunities they choose to see. That is what saps their energy. They are not convinced of their unique value for changing the world.

Internal Conversations

Much is written and said about self-talk, those messages we tell ourselves. However, it's more than just the talk. It is the internal conversations where we create our identity, self-concept, and self-image. That makes our internal conversations vitally important.

Most people tend to be too critical, demanding perfection or a higher standard than is reasonable. We use guilt and shame to punish ourselves, thinking we deserve it.

Stop it.

This is very harmful. Instead, create a healthy self-concept and self-esteem by looking at yourself honestly. That means considering your strengths and weaknesses. Avoid focusing too much on the negative because you don't want to dismiss your own power. You also don't want to inflate your ego by only looking at your strengths. That makes you arrogant. Be humble but confident. Be willing to admit when you are wrong.

Admitting you are wrong is powerful. But don't always fall on your sword. Be honest. Understand who is legitimately to blame. Take your share of the blame but not anyone else's share.

Use those guilt messages to learn from mistakes and then let it go. That is right don't carry the guilt messages with you. Let them go. Guilt's only purpose is to teach from a mistake and to correct character. Once you have learned the lessons, let it go. Even when you make the same mistakes repeatedly, as we all do with certain weaknesses, don't allow guilt to become shame. Guilt says, "I did something wrong." Shame says, "I'm a bad person."

Eliminate all shame messages. Never say, "Shame on me." Those messages destroy your power by eroding your confidence and self-worth.

Know your unique value. Then counter each negative message from your inner critic with positive, powerful language that rebuts it. Refuting the argument floods our brain with positive messages but also helps to rewire our brain. Negative messages literally leave a rut in our brain where the default is negativity. Powerful messages re-engineers our thinking by forging new paths that are positive. Changing that mental habit will take time, energy, and the hard work of discipline and repetition but it yields great power. This process will transform your self-concept, self-imagine, and self-esteem. Work to leverage the power of your brain.

Conversations with Others

You are reading this book because you want to leverage your power to seize your ultimate opportunity. Keep that focus in every conversation. To do what you never imagined possible, you must become who you ultimately want to become. That means, take the high road by finding the best in people and celebrating it. Read Dale Carnegie's classic *How to Win Friends and Influence People*. He wisely suggests being interested in others. That is the way to make friends with anyone. I like to say that we should then celebrate them, what they have done and who they have become. Imagine how that pivots your power and helps you get what you ultimately want.

Focus on important matters. Engage in small talk as necessary to build relationships but don't linger there. Be known as one who knows their priorities and adheres to them.

At the same time, be compassionate. Be concerned for those who are legitimately hurting. However, be careful to avoid getting drug into their whirlwind of drama. Help those who are willing to help themselves. In the process, you create a great reputation as a giver while endearing others to you while doing what is right. Others will want to connect with a person of integrity like that.

At the end of this chapter, you will find a section you will find a list of valuable power tips to use in conversations. Space doesn't permit a discussion of each.

Powerful Language

Our words hold the power to create and destroy. Knowing the best word to use in the right situation is like being impeccably dressed. People are impressed when we can articulate exactly what we mean without going over their head.

That requires understanding how words swell with meaning at certain times and then empty. They are the current trendy word used in headlines but then they become like yesterday's news. The term "family" had its moment in the sun in 1992 after Dan Quayle mentioned Murphy Brown and "Family Values." He used it as a filtering term to talk about issues most wouldn't engage with. As the Republican Vice-President running in a re-election, the general public would engage about a popular sit-com character but not about the political ideology of property and equality. Quayle was mocked but succeeded in starting a conversation that engaged his political base.

You can do the same. Find filtering words that generate a conversation otherwise seen as repulsive or boring. Instead of politics, take a tip from Jonathan Haidt in *The Righteous Mind*. Talk about values instead of polarized political issues. Talk about care or fairness. Engage others about loyalty or authority. Instead of talking about religion, you can engage on what is most important. Use the finesse of your vocabulary and thinking to discuss values instead of issues.

Also, discuss the process instead of polarizing issues or blame. Few people will pick a fight with someone exploring foundational values. They will argue, get upset, and divide based on political policies or proposed laws.

While language is powerful and definitely important to leverage, don't become the grammar police. No one likes them. No one wants to be corrected, especially in a public discussion. Correcting someone shows an arrogance. While they think it makes them more powerful, it only decreases their status. The power tip is to let it go. There is no way you will look any better if you counter them in that situation. It doesn't mean they are right but don't let them bring you down to their level.

In the following section, you will find several lists of power communication tips. We begin with character because being leads to action. Just doing is being obedience in an outside-in fashion However, when you are becoming your best self, you take actions based on an inside-out model. You aren't doing them to obey but because they work to help you unleash your ultimate potential. Allow these power tips to serve as your Pivotal Communication Checklist.

Checklist: Pivotal Power Communication

<u>Character</u>
- ☐ Be authentic.
- ☐ Own your unique value. In other words, be confident in who you are.
- ☐ Don't pretend to be more than you are.
- ☐ Laugh at yourself but don't criticize yourself openly.
- ☐ Be good.
- ☐ Be positive.
- ☐ Be compassionate.
- ☐ Be professional.

- ☐ Celebrate others.
- ☐ Know your limits.
- ☐ Associate with good people.
- ☐ Build authentic relationships with powerful people.
- ☐ Don't become the butt of jokes.
- ☐ When in conflict, be the better person. Take the high road.
- ☐ Become the great idea person who thinks bigger and reaches higher.
- ☐ Be responsible.
- ☐ Take the right action at the perfect time to exceed expectations.

<u>Public Speaking</u>
- ☐ Make eye contact.
- ☐ Listen far more than you speak.
- ☐ Follow the E.F. Hutton rule: be concise but say a lot.
- ☐ Be positive.
- ☐ Be direct but subtle.
- ☐ Develop a good vocabulary.
- ☐ Use precise words.
- ☐ Never use slang.
- ☐ Eliminate vulgar or swear words.
- ☐ Eliminate filler words ("Um" "Ah" etc.)
- ☐ Develop a lower your vocal tone
- ☐ Speak softly when upset or making an important point. (as opposed to raising your voice.)
- ☐ Don't raise your voice at the end of a sentence.
- ☐ Work diligently to remember names.
- ☐ Use their name when speaking with them.
- ☐ Don't complain. Become a problem solver. Offer a solution.
- ☐ Raise issues in private conversations instead of in a group, meeting, or in public.
- ☐ Avoid controversial subjects like politics and religion. Leave them for private conversations.

- ☐ Don't get involved in meaningless conversations. You don't have to have an opinion or voice it if it doesn't immediately concern you.
- ☐ When questioning whether to say something, don't.
- ☐ Only speak when your voice is needed.

Listening
- ☐ Listen first to understand
- ☐ Listen to understand from their perspective
- ☐ Listen to feel their pain (What is currently hurting them physically, mentally, or emotionally?)
- ☐ Affirm the other person's perspective, value, and experience.
- ☐ Think before speaking.
- ☐ Consider the short and long-term effects before responding.
- ☐ Find something you can relate to with everyone you meet.

Nonverbal
- ☐ Smile but not constantly.
- ☐ Be clean.
- ☐ Be neat.
- ☐ Be punctual but not too early.
- ☐ Sit at the head of the table when you are in charge.
- ☐ Sit at the foot of the table when possible.
- ☐ If the first two are not appropriate, sit at the side on the corner near the head.
- ☐ Keep gestures between your waist and shoulders.
- ☐ Dress slightly better than your audience or team, but not gaudy.
- ☐ Keep your chin up.
- ☐ Refrain from touching your face unless listening.
- ☐ Always display good posture.
- ☐ Know which colors look good on you.
- ☐ Know and wear the style appropriate for the occasion.
- ☐ Build your brand through your attire.
- ☐ Take notes in meetings.

- ☐ Use the power stance in appropriate settings. (See Amy Cuddy's on TED.com)

CONCLUSION

You hold the power to your future.
You hold the power to dream.
You hold the power to pivot.
You hold the power to choose.

You choose to be powerful or weak.
You choose to be successful or a failure.
You choose to pursue the ultimate or settle for ordinary.

You choose whether to hoard or leverage power.
You choose to compete or collaborate.
You choose to remain quiet, or to speak up, and share your ideas.
You choose to listen, or to speak.

You have the choice to pivot.
You have the choice to think bigger.
You have the choice to reach higher.

In the end, you have the power to do what you never imagined.
You have the power to seize your ultimate opportunity.
You might even have the power to do what no one thought possible.

Leverage that power.

Loren Murfield, Ph.D.

Pivotal Power

REFERENCES

Carnegie, D. *How to Win Friends & Influence People*. (1936) Pocket Books. New York.

Cuddy, A. (www.TED.com) https://www.ted.com/talks/amy_cuddy_your_body_language_may_shape_who_you_are?language=en

Frankl, V.E. *Man's Search for Meaning*. (1984) Washington Square Books. New York.

Good Therapy. https://www.goodtherapy.org/famous-psychologists/viktor-frankl.html

Grant, A. *Give and Take* (2013) Penguin. New York.

Grant, A. Think Again. (2021). Viking. New York.

Gregersen, Eric. (ed.) "Energy" (2019, Mar. 25) Encyclopedia Britannica, https://www.britannica.com/science/energy

Haidt, J. *The Righteous Mind* (2012) Vintage Books. New York.

Hawkins, David, R. (2002) *Power vs Force*. Hay House. Carlsbad, Ca.

Kim, W and Mongaue, R. *Blue Oceans Strategy* (2005) Harvard Business School Press, Boston.

Lafair, S. Don't Bring it To Work. (2009) Jossey-Bass. San Francisco.

May, Rollo. *Power and Innocence* (1972) W.W. Norton & Co., New York

Morris, Donald. "Opportunity" (2006). Prometheus Books, Amherst, NY

Murfield, Lisa & Loren. *The ROI of Compassion* (2018)

Murfield, Loren, *Chevettes to Corvettes: Unleashing the Ultimate Small Business* (2018)
Murfield, Loren, *Making More Money in Tough Times* (2018)
Murfield, Loren, *The Prize Inside* (anticipated late 2019)
Nye, Joseph *The Future of Power* (2011), Public Affairs, New York
Nye, Joseph, *The Powers to Lead* (2008), Oxford Press, New York
Nye, Joseph, *Soft Power*, 2004, Public Affairs, New York
Pittman, C. & Karle, E. *Rewire Your Anxious Brain*, (2005) New Harbinger Productions, Inc. Oakland, CA
Raven, B. H. & French, J. (1959). The bases of social power. In D. Cartwright (Ed.), Studies in social power (pp. 150-167). Ann Arbor, MI: Institute for Social Research.
Robins, T. (https://www.tonyrobbins.com/stories/unleash-the-power/overcoming-fear-in-5-steps/)
Ruiz, D. The Four Agreements. (1997) Amber-Allen Publishing. San Rafael, CA.
Sinek, Simon, "Why Great Leaders Inspire Action" (2009, Sept.) TED Talk, www.ted.com
TonyRobbins.com (https://www.tonyrobbins.com/stories/unleash-the-power/overcoming-fear-in-5-steps/)
Wikipedia.com. "Energy" (2019, Mar. 25) https://en.wikipedia.org/wiki/Energy
Yahoo.com (https://www.yahoo.com/now/garth-brooks-says-freddie-mercury-160537002.html)

Definitions from www.dictionary.com and www.merriam-webster.com/

PIVOTAL LIVING AND WORKING SERIES

Available at www.PivotalLiving.org and www.BetterYou.TV and Amazon.com

MEDITATIONS from the NATIONAL PARKS SERIES

Books to be released in 2024

Available at www.PivotalLiving.org and www.BetterYou.TV and Amazon.com

VIDEO COURSES and SERIES

Fundamentals for Your Success
   Building Your Competence
   Building Your Reputation
   Building Your Confidence
   Building Your Skills
   Building Your Leadership
Pivotal Listening: Building Better Skills to Create Your Personal and Business and Breakthrough
5 Steps to Find Your Unique Value
Doc's Daily Video Series
   Resurrection Sunday
   Motivational Monday
   Think Bigger Tuesday
   Why Not Reach Higher Wednesday
   Try Running Thursday
   Friday Meditations from the National Parks
   Strategic Saturday
Living 100% A.L.I.V.E.

www.BetterYou.TV

COMING SOON

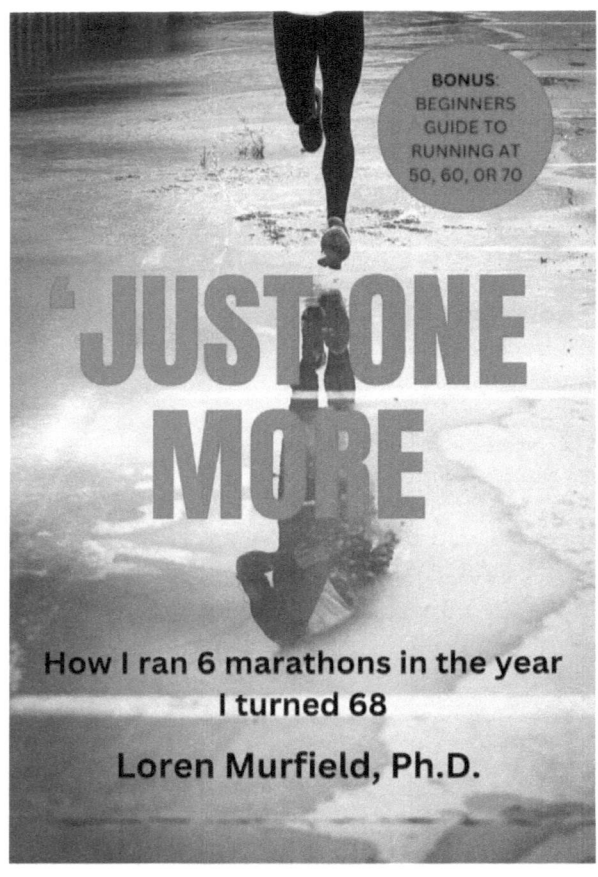

ABOUT the AUTHOR

Dr. Loren Murfield is an innovative thinker who serves as an Executive Coach, Author, and Speaker. He holds a Ph.D. in Communication Studies from the University of Nebraska and has authored over 40 books and multiple online and in-person courses. His books address business, professional, and personal development. Working with entrepreneurs and organizational leaders, he challenges their thinking to see cutting-edge opportunities.

He has also written and acted in a movie short, wrote, as well as staged and acted in eight plays. In 2022-23, he ran 6 marathons in the year he turned 68. He speaks to local, state, and international audiences in person and virtually.

Life is indeed far too short to settle for the ordinary limitations others place upon us.

Websites: www.BetterYou.TV
            www.MurfieldCoaching.com
            www.PivotalLiving.com
            www.PivotalAgent.com

Email: Loren@MurfieldCoaching.com

www.ingramcontent.com/pod-product-compliance
Lightning Source LLC
Chambersburg PA
CBHW031424210526
45464CB00005B/2035